Easy KEYTAB Method

Christmas Songs

Written & Method By:
John McCarthy

Supervising Editor: John McCarthy
Music Arrangements: Damiano Christian & John McCarthy
Music Transcribing & Engraving: Damiano Christian
Production Manager: John McCarthy
Layout, Graphics, & Design: Jimmy Rutkowski
Copy Editors:
Cathy McCarthy & John McCarthy

Cover Art Direction & Design:
Jimmy Rutkowski

ISBN: 979-8-218-48991-5
Produced by McCarthy Publishing

Table of Contents

Sing Along Versions

About the Author

John Frederick McCarthy is a musician, author, educator and creator of the Rock House Method system of learning. Since 2001, The Rock House Method has sold more than three million instructional programs of which McCarthy writes, composes, and demonstrates in. McCarthy has developed a curriculum for learning to play music that covers guitar, piano, ukulele, drums, bass guitar, singing, children's early music development and music theory. Currently he has authored over 60 instructional method books and 58 instructional DVDs. In addition to his own instructional books and programs John has worked with many of the greatest musicians in the world creating personal instruction programs featuring the Rock House Method. John also is the founder/owner of the Rock House School of Music since 1981and is franchising and opening locations across America. In 2020 John McCarthy was awarded a patent for his revolutionary new way to read piano music called KEYTAB. The KEYTAB Piano system comes with a "KEYTAB Note Strip" and uses a unique color-coded sheet music to allow players to learn songs quickly and easily.

How to Use this Book

Dive into the musical wonderland of this book, where each song comes with a double dose of fun! You'll find a "Full Melody" version and a super cool "Sing Along" version. The Sing Along one? Oh, it's like having your very own musical sidekick – complete with chords, so you can belt out tunes or jam with your family and pals. Lyrics? Yup, we've got them covered for you in every song. But wait, there's more! Head over to KeyTabMusic.com, where you can catch video tutorials for each song, making it a breeze to conquer those tricky parts. Get ready for a musical adventure that's not just awesome but also packed with all the help you need to become a rockstar in no time!

How to Read KEYTAB

Get ready for the awesome world of KEYTAB – it's the magical key that makes playing cool songs and chords on the piano super easy! This modern music reading system is a shortcut to letting you groove to your favorite tunes in no time at all.

Now, here's the lowdown on KEYTAB: Imagine the staff on your sheet music is like a road, and right in the middle, there's a count bar telling you the beat of the song. The top part is for your right hand, and the bottom part is for your left hand. The letters tell you the note's name, and the colors show which part of the keyboard to play. Grab your KEYTAB Note Strip, slap it behind your piano keys, and match the colors – easy, right? Oh, and those numbers after each note? They're like your musical GPS, guiding your fingers where to go. It's as simple as that! Now go on, have a blast playing your favorite songs!

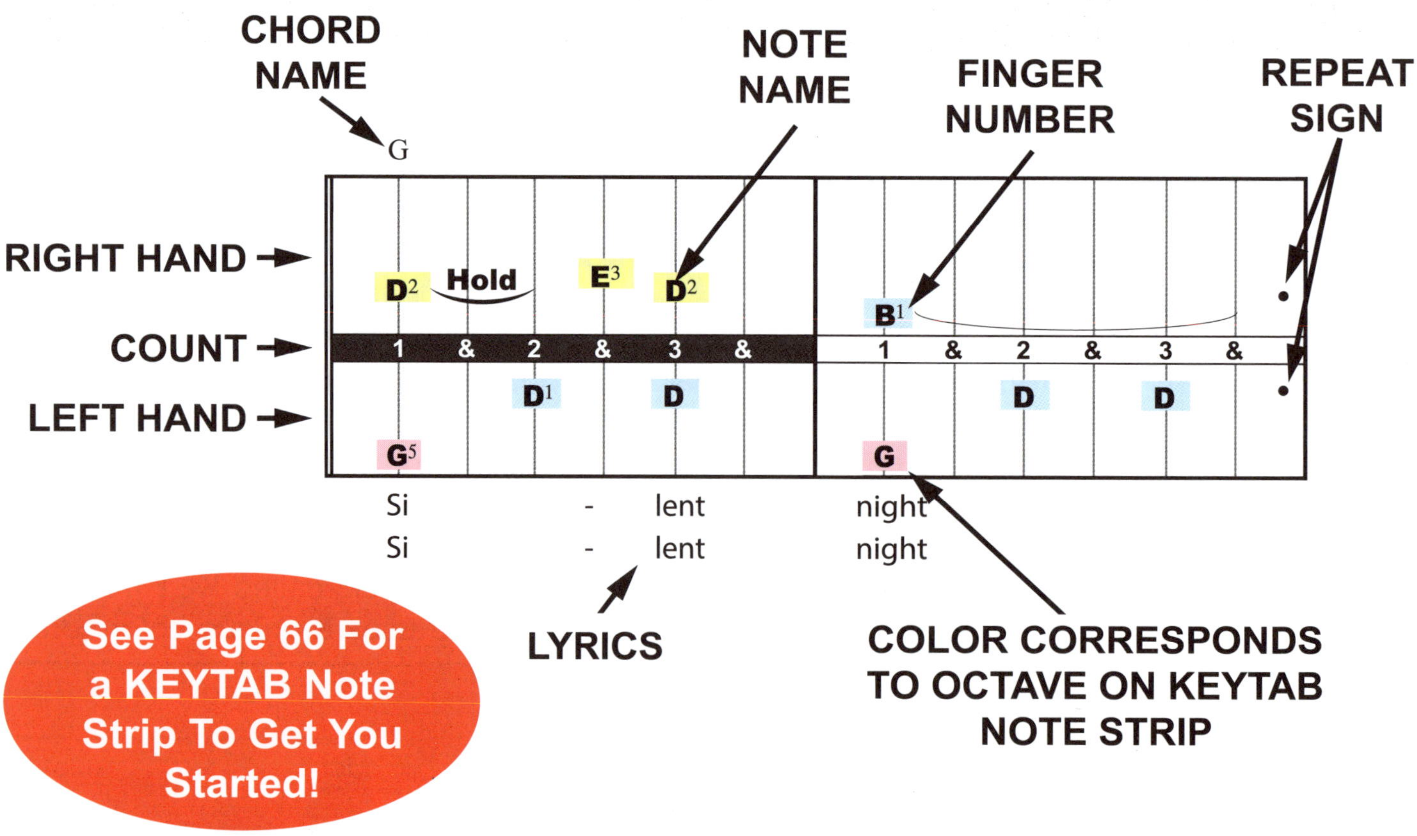

See Page 66 For a KEYTAB Note Strip To Get You Started!

Repeat Signs, Let Ring Slurs and Finger Numbers

Within the songs featured in this book, you will encounter two common notations: repeat signs and hold slurs. A repeat sign directs you to go back and replay the same section before progressing beyond the sign to the next part of the music. If a section needs to be repeated multiple times, you will find a number above the final repeat sign indicating how many repetitions are required. If no number is specified, repeat the section once and then proceed to the following part.

Hold slurs are used to signify that the key(s) being played should be sustained, allowing the notes to ring for the specified duration indicated by the count. For instance, in the first song of this book, "Silent Night," the first note D is played with the second finger on the 1 count and then sustained for the "& 2 " count, then the E note is played with the third finger. In the second measure, the note B is played on the 1 count and should be held for the "& 2 & 3 &" counts.

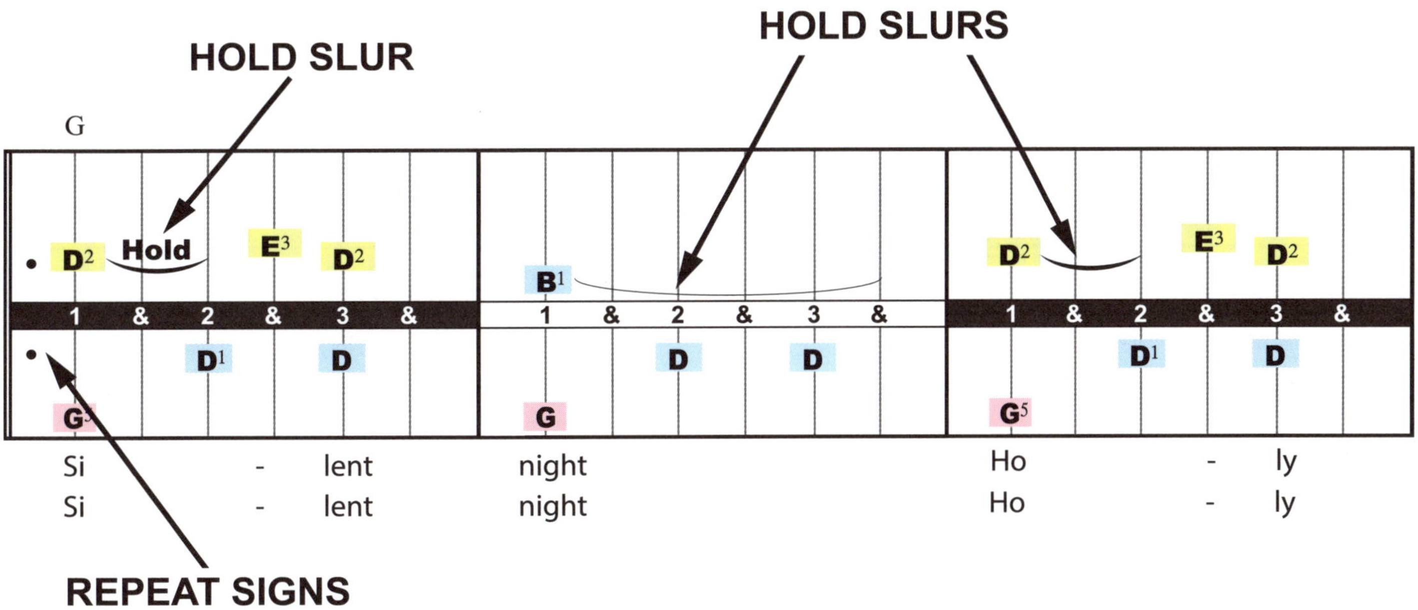

Finger Numbers

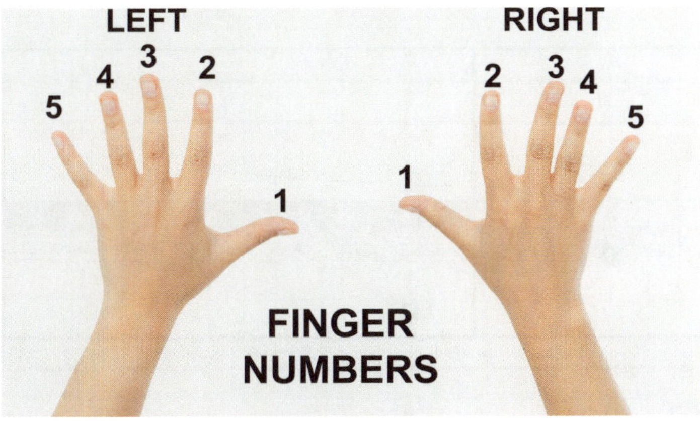

Access Your Video Lessons

Included with this book are video tutorials for each song. These tutorials go through each song slowly with close-up views and then each song is played at full speed. To access your video lessons go to **www.KeyTabMusic.com**.

Silent Night

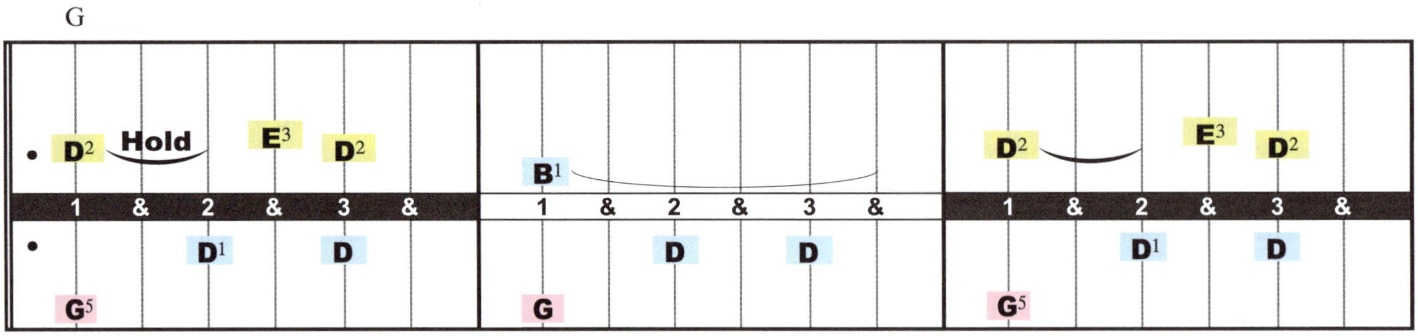

Si - lent night Ho - ly
Si - lent night Ho - ly

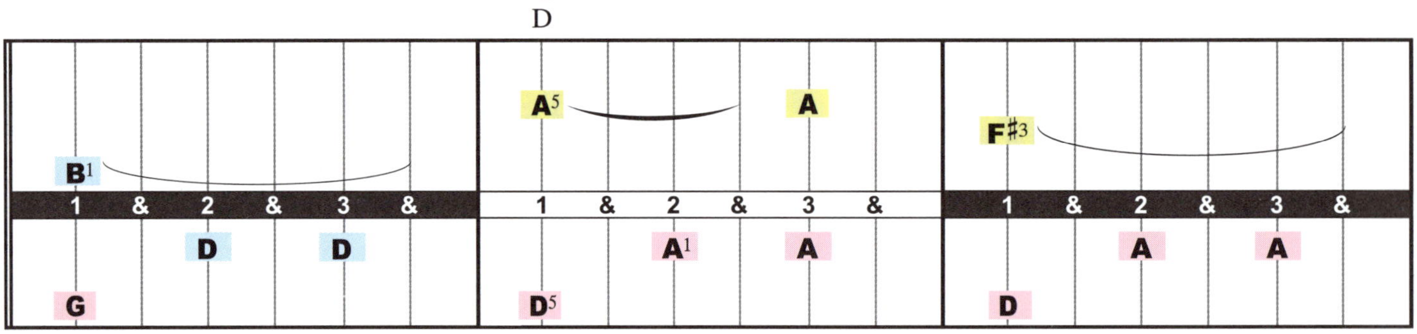

night All is calm
night She - pherds quake

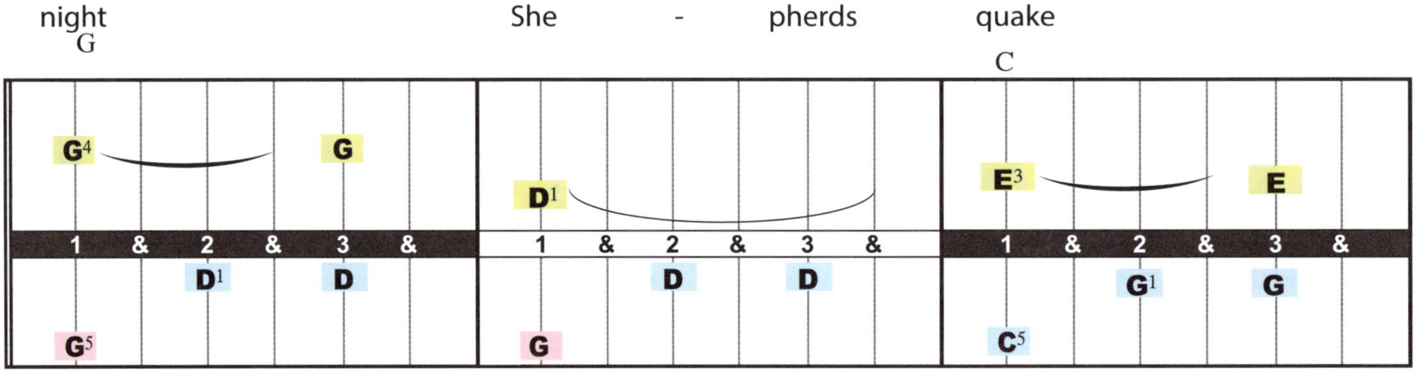

All is bright Round young
At the sight Glor - ies

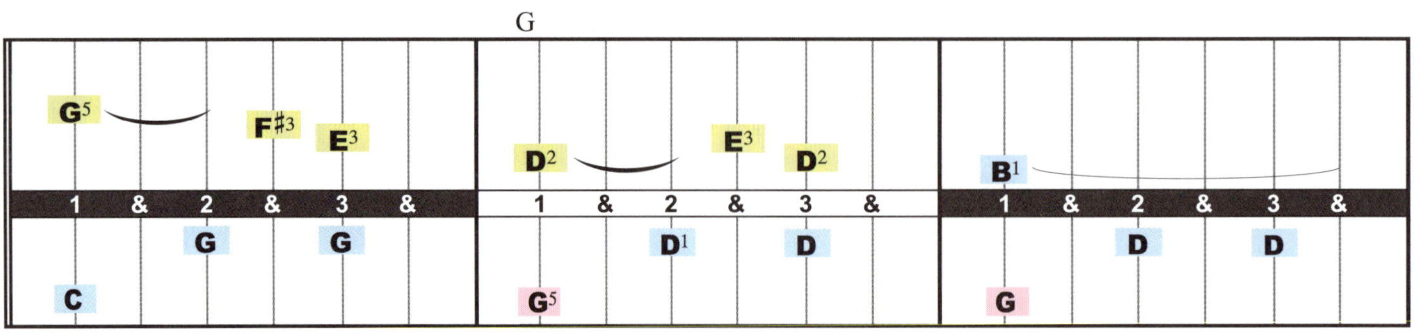

vir - gin Moth - er and child
stre - am from Hea - ven a far

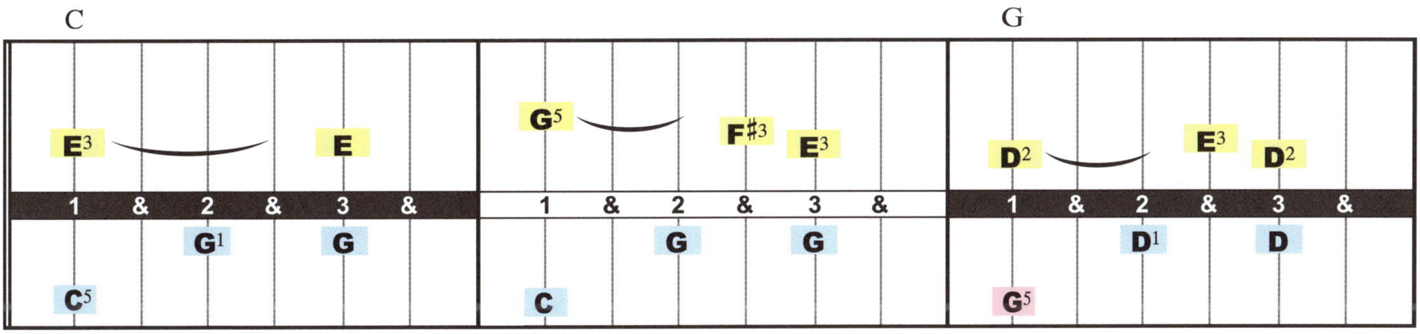

Ho - ly in - fant so ten - der and
Hea - venly ho - sts sing A - lle - lu -

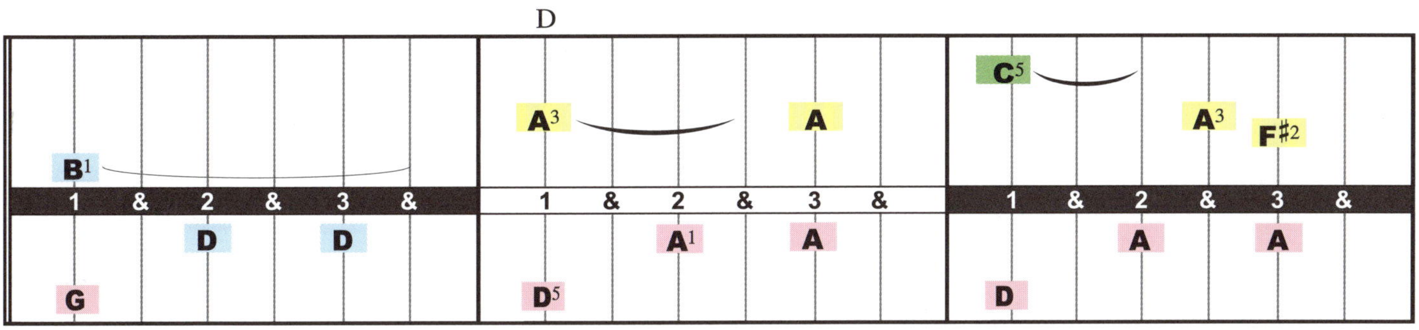

mild Sleep in hea - ven ly
ia Christ the sa - vior is

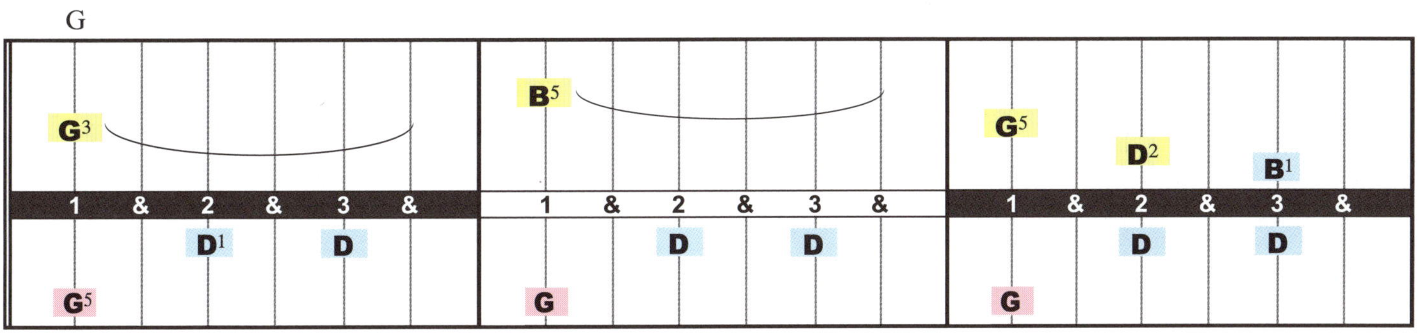

Pea - ce Sle - ep in
Bo - rn Chri - st the

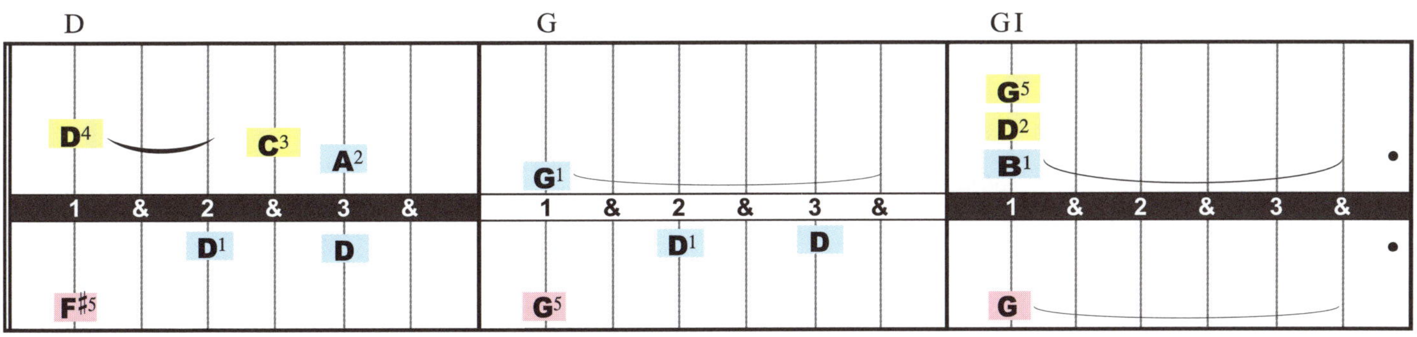

Hea - ven ly Peace
Sav - ior is Born

Jingle Bells

C

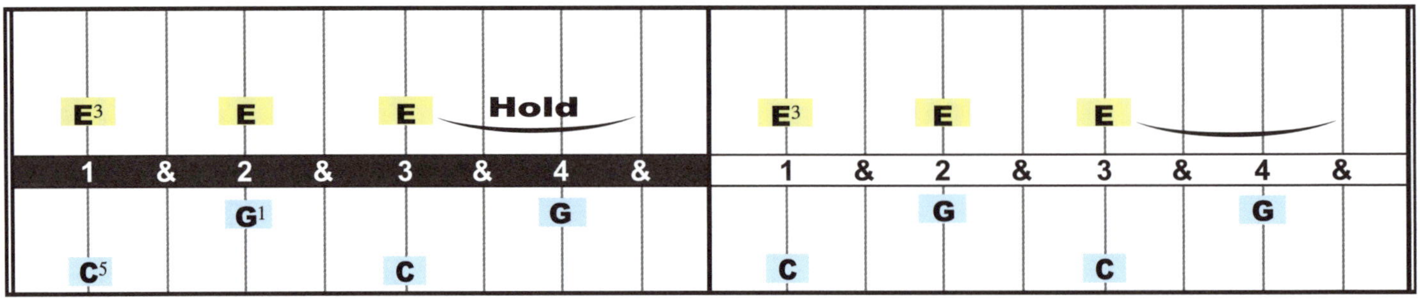

Jin - gle bells Jin - gle bells

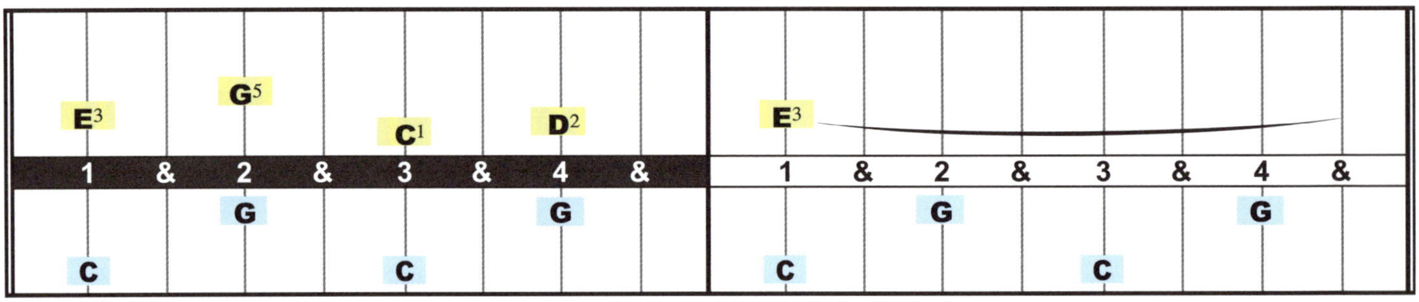

Jin- gle all the way

F C

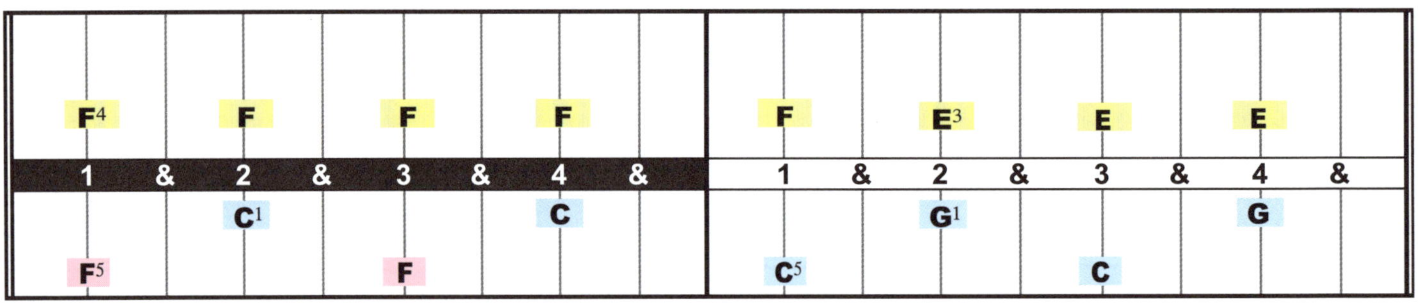

oh, what fun it is to ride in a

1. G7

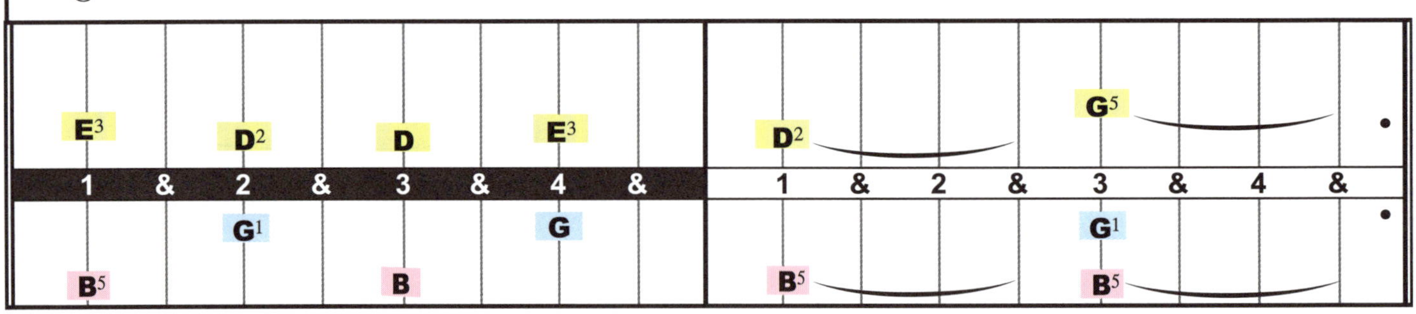

one horse o - pen sleigh hey!

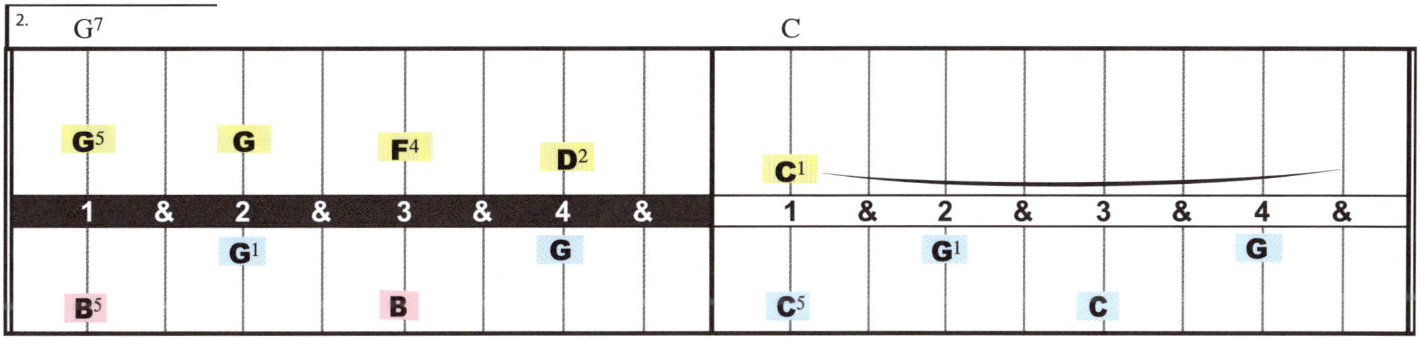

One Horse o - pen sleigh

Verse

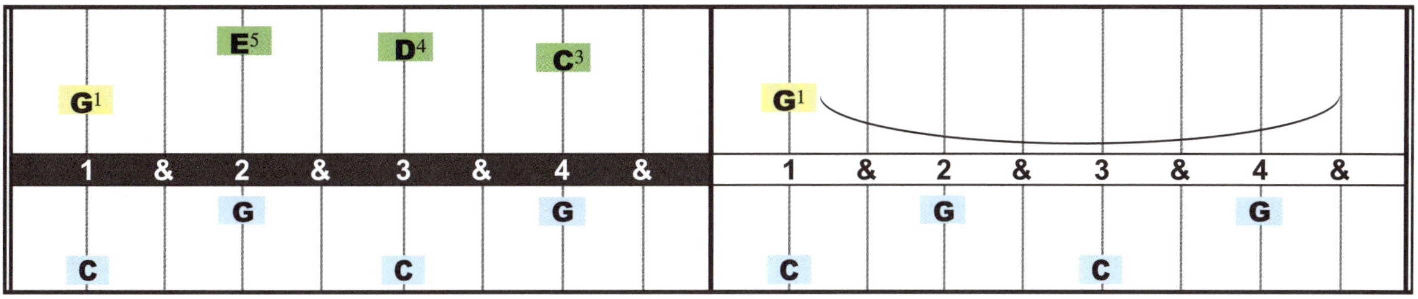

Dash - ing thru the snow on a
Bells on bob tail ring

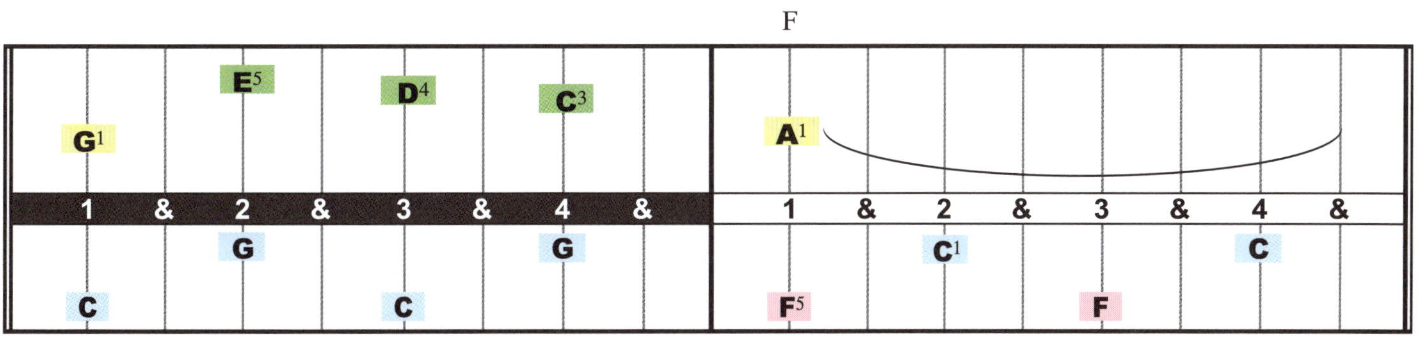

one - Horse o - pen sleigh
mak - ing spir - its bright what

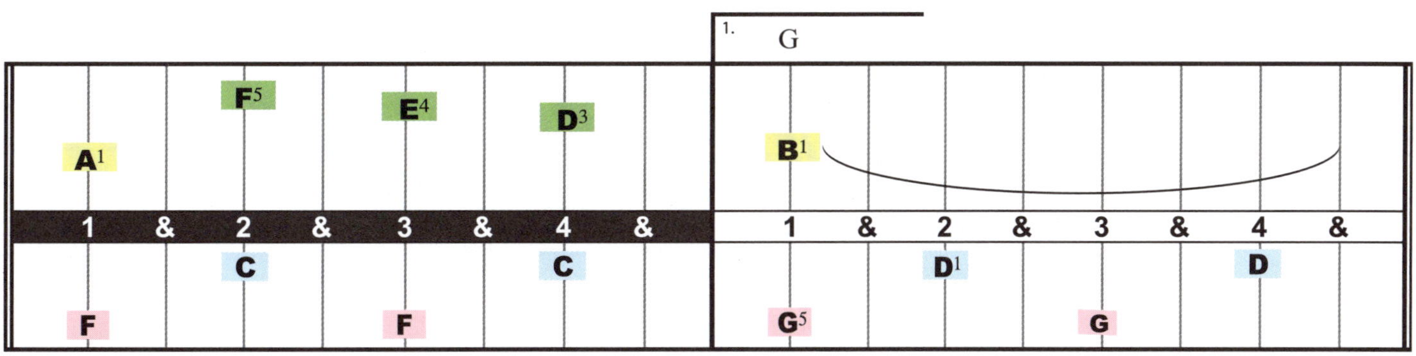

O'er the fields we go
fun it is to

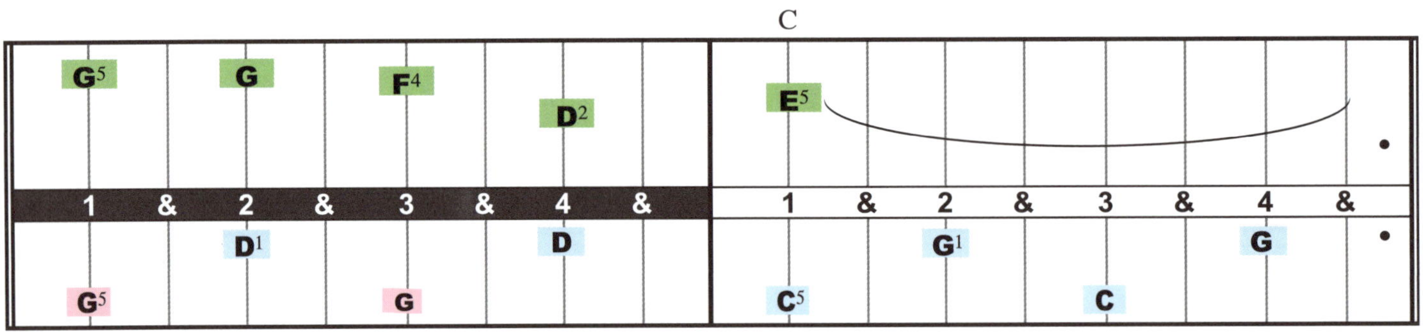

Laugh - ing all the way

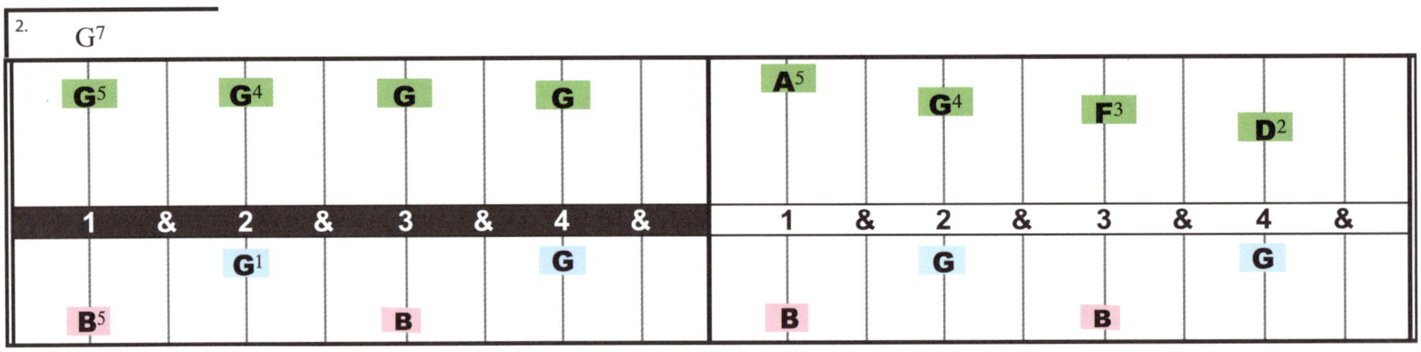

laugh and sing a sleigh - ing song to -

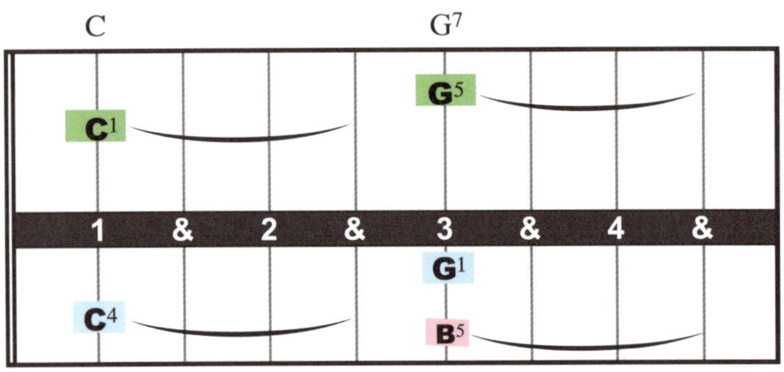

night oh!

Good King Wenceslas

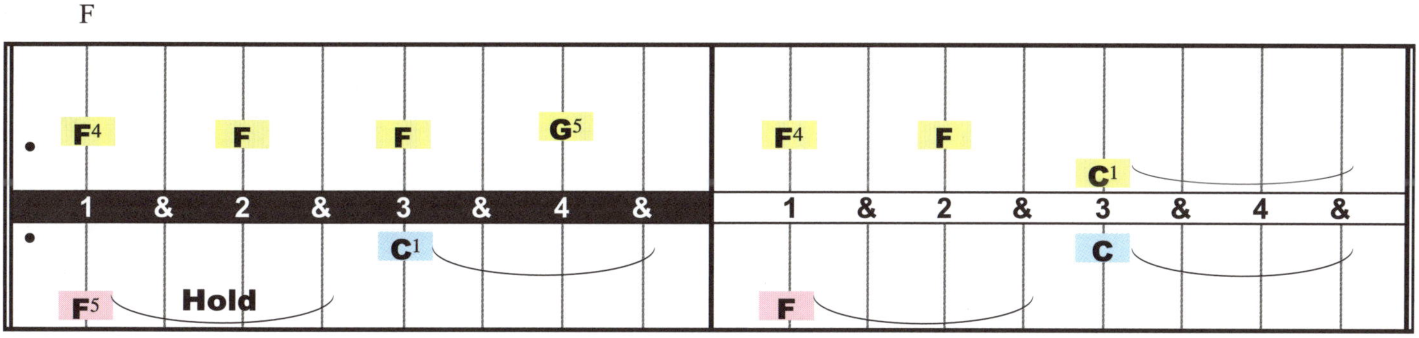

Good King Wen - ces - las Looked out
When the snow lay round a - bout

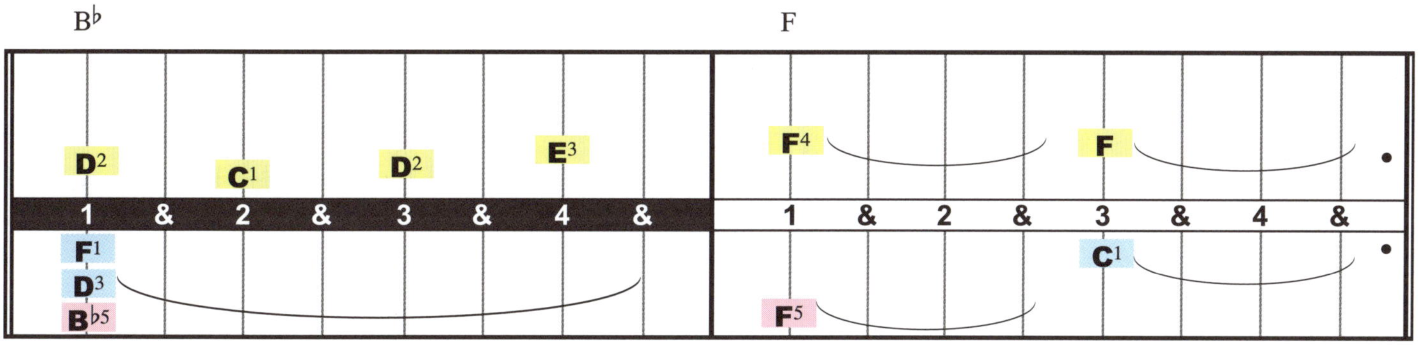

on the feast of Ste - phen
deep and crisp and e - ven

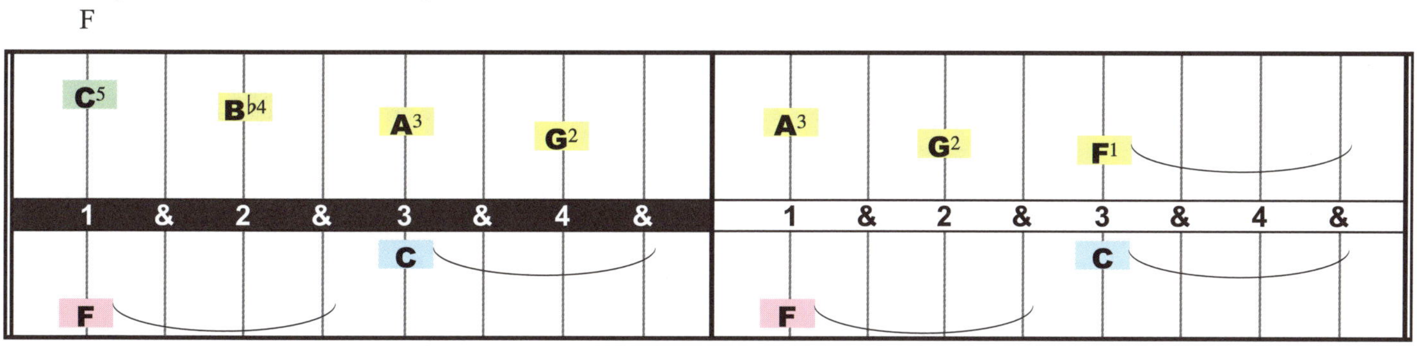

bright - ly shown the moon that night

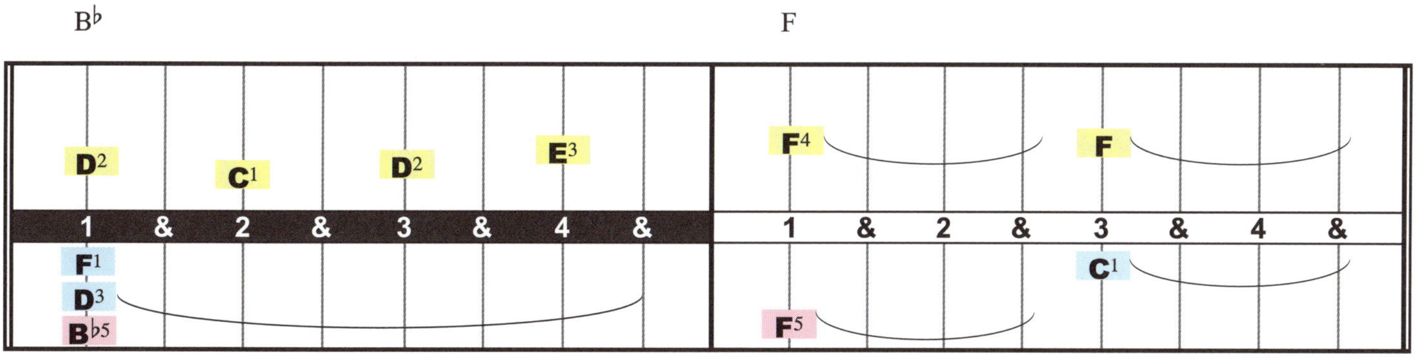

though the frost was cru - el

F

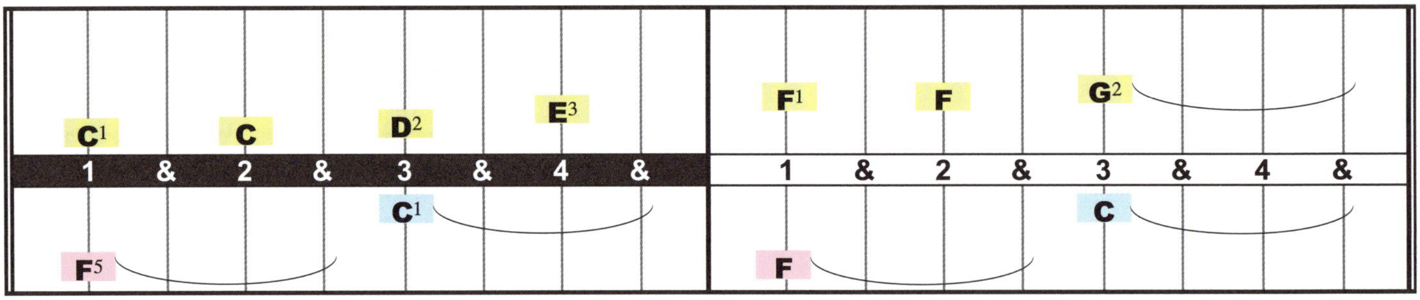

when a poor man came in sight

C B♭

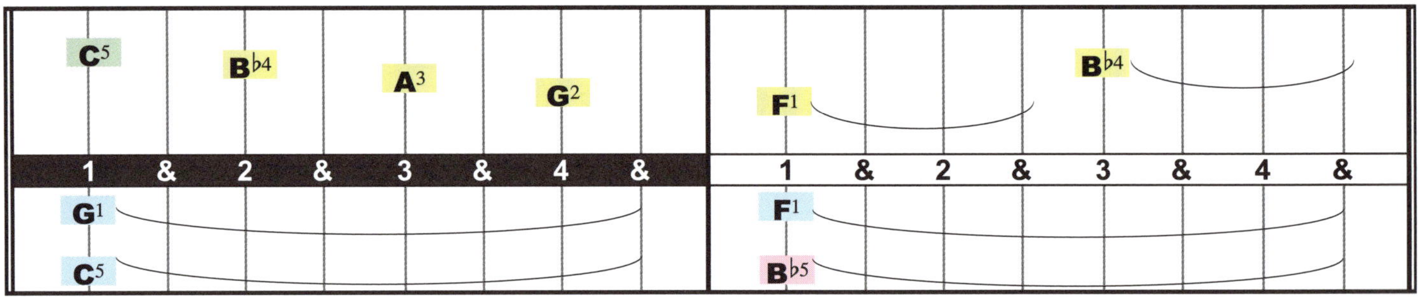

gathe - ring win - ter Fu -

F

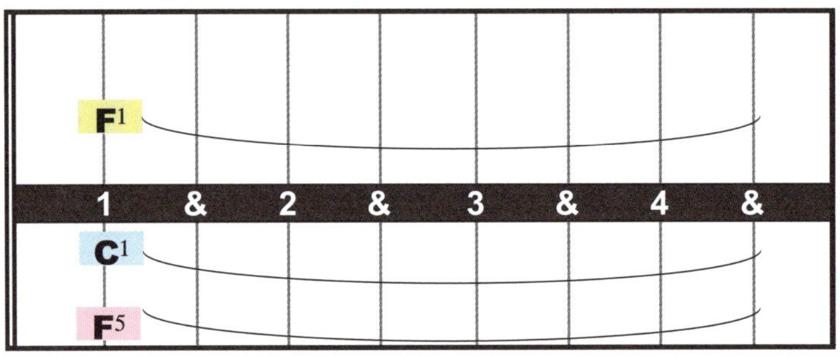

el

Verse 2

Hither, page, and stand by me,
If thou knowst it, telling
Yonder peasant, who is he?
Where and what his dwelling?
Sire, he lives a good league hence,
Underneath the mountain
Right against the forest fence
By Saint Agnes fountain.

Verse 3

Bring me flesh and bring me wine
Bring me pine logs hither
Thou and I shall see him dine
When we bear them thither.
Page and monarch, forth they went
Forth they went together
Through the rude winds wild lament
And the bitter weather

Verse 4

Sire, the night is darker now
And the wind blows stronger
Fails my heart, I know not how
I can go no longer.
Mark my footsteps, good my page
Tread thou in them boldly
Thou shall find the winters rage
Freeze thy blood less coldly.

Verse 5

In his masters step he trod
Where the snow lay dinted
Heat was in the very sod
Which the Saint had printed
Therefore, Christian men, be sure
Wealth or rank possessing
Ye, who now will bless the poor
Shall yourselves find blessing.

Santa Claus is Coming to Town

Verse

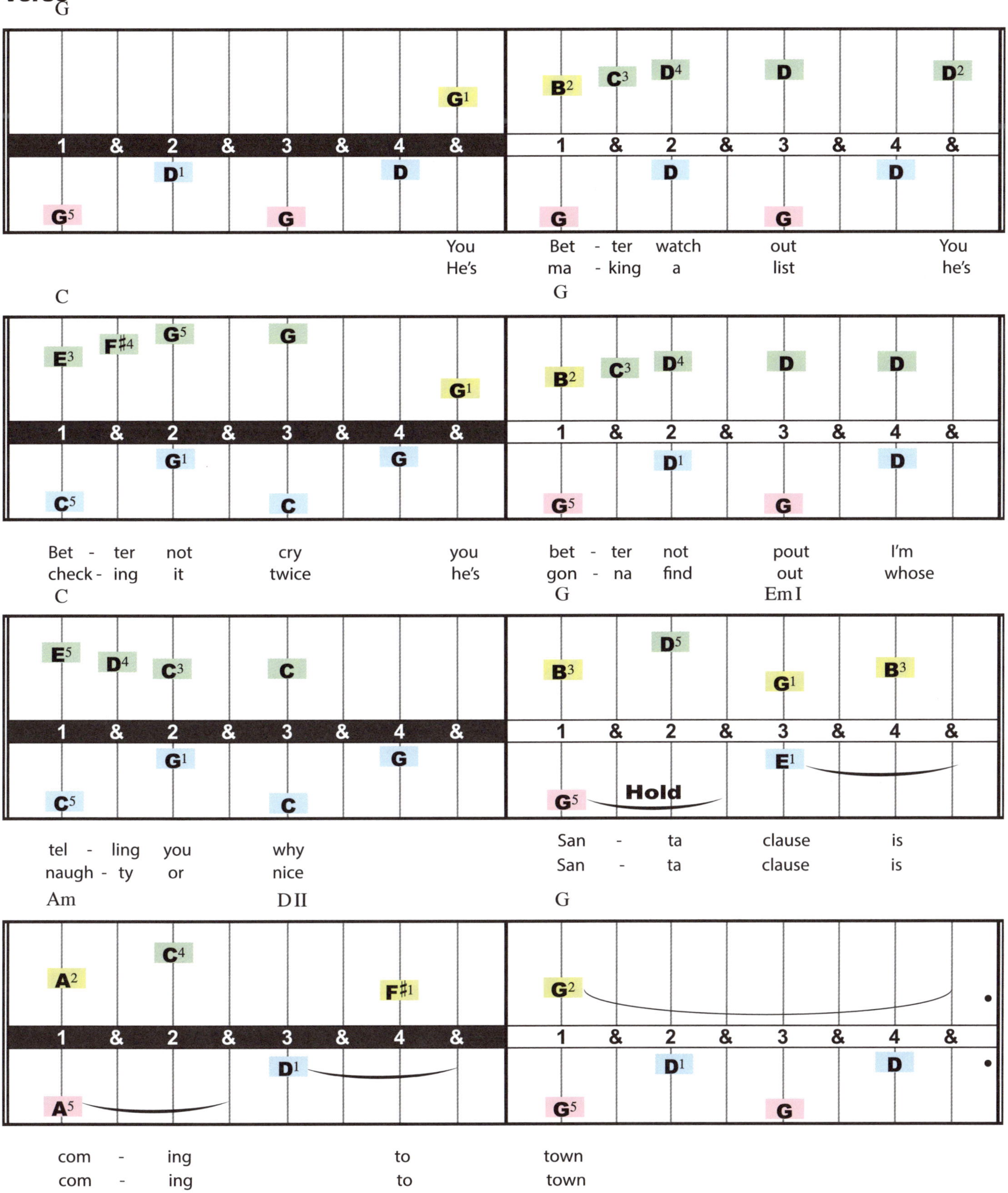

Bridge

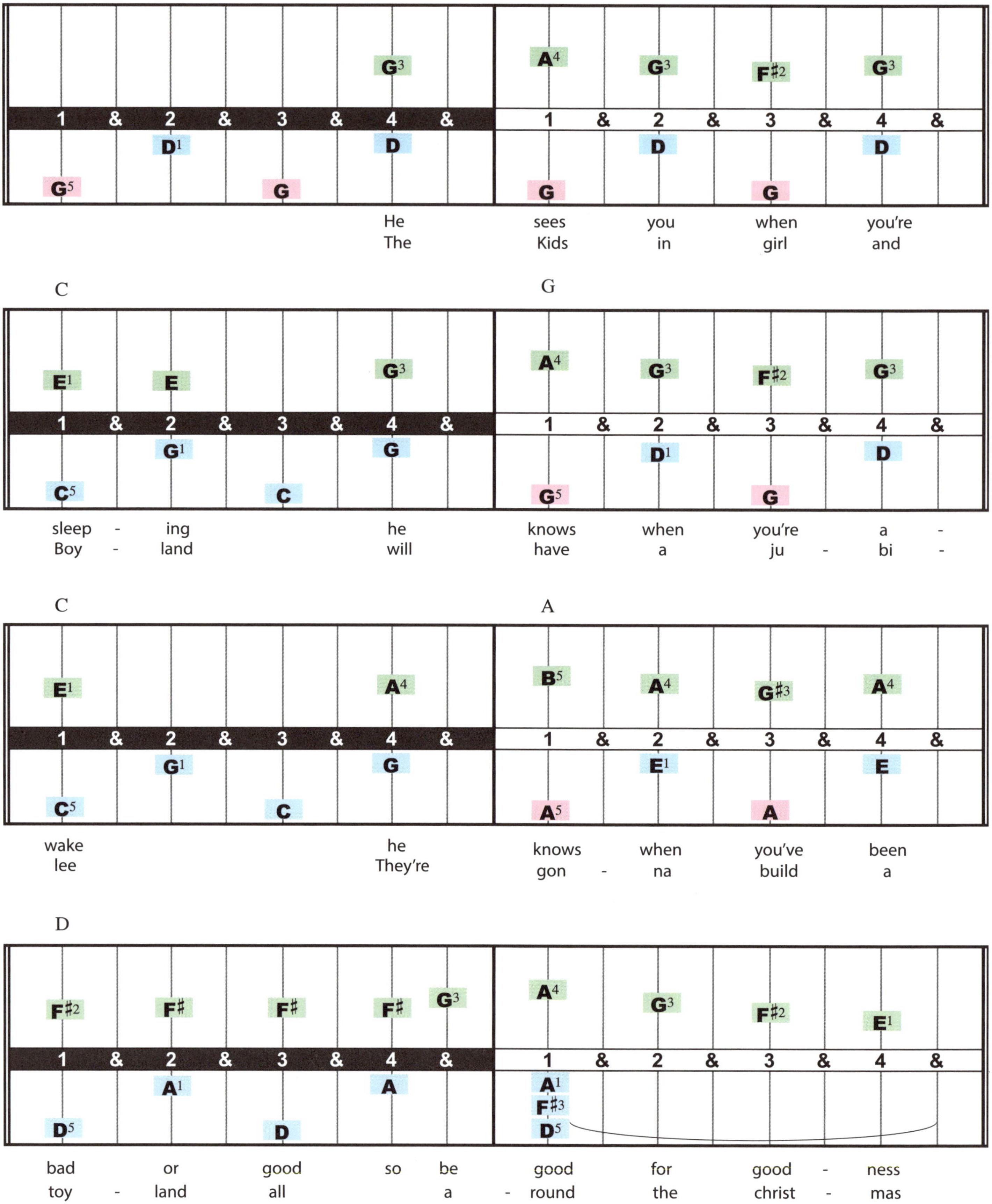
G
He sees you when you're
The Kids in girl and
C
G
sleep - ing he knows when you're a -
Boy - land will have a ju - bi -
C
A
wake he knows when you've been
lee They're gon - na build a
D
bad or good so be good for good - ness
toy - land all a - round the christ - mas

G

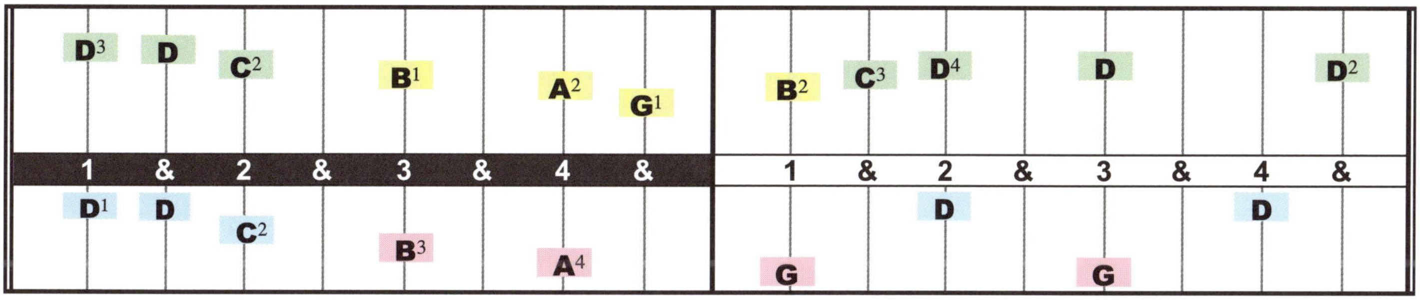

Sake so You Bet - ter watch out You

tree so

Chorus

C G

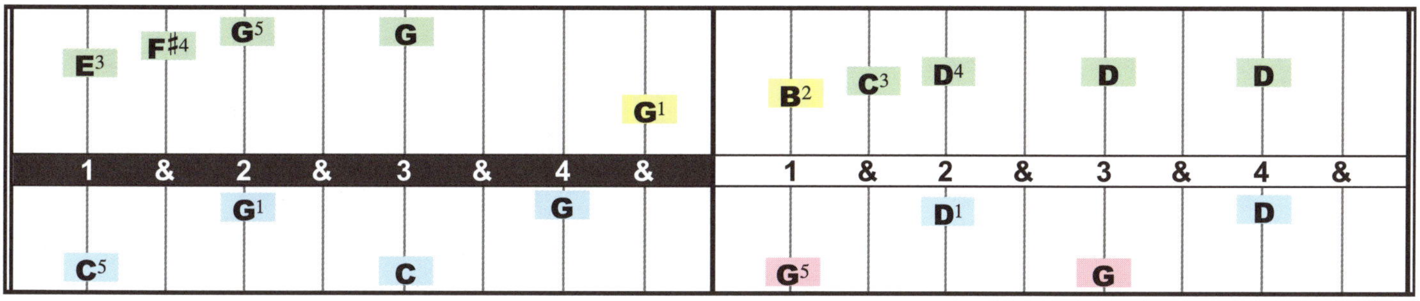

Bet - ter not cry you bet - ter not pout I'm

C G EmI

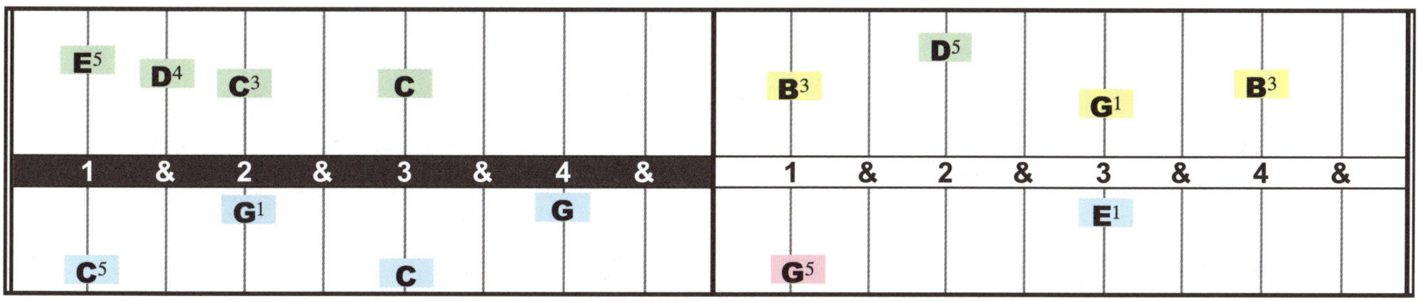

tel - ling you why San - ta clause is

Am DII G

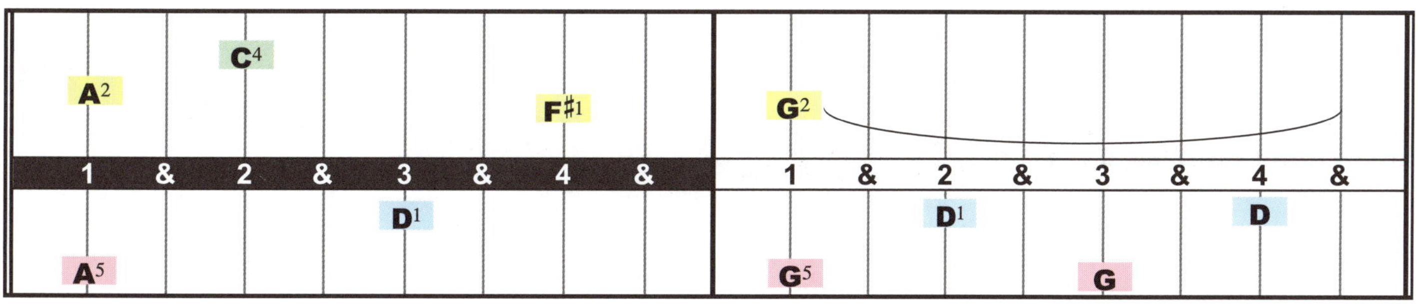

com - ing to town

Structure

Verse - Verse - Bridge - Chorus - Verse
Verse - Bridge - Chorus - Bridge - Choruse 2x

Verse 2
Little tin horns, little tin drums
Rudy-toot-toot and rummy tum tums
Santa Claus is comin' to town

Verse 3
And curly head dolls that cuddle and coo
Elephants, boats and kiddy cars too
Santa Claus is comin' to town

We Wish You a Merry Christmas

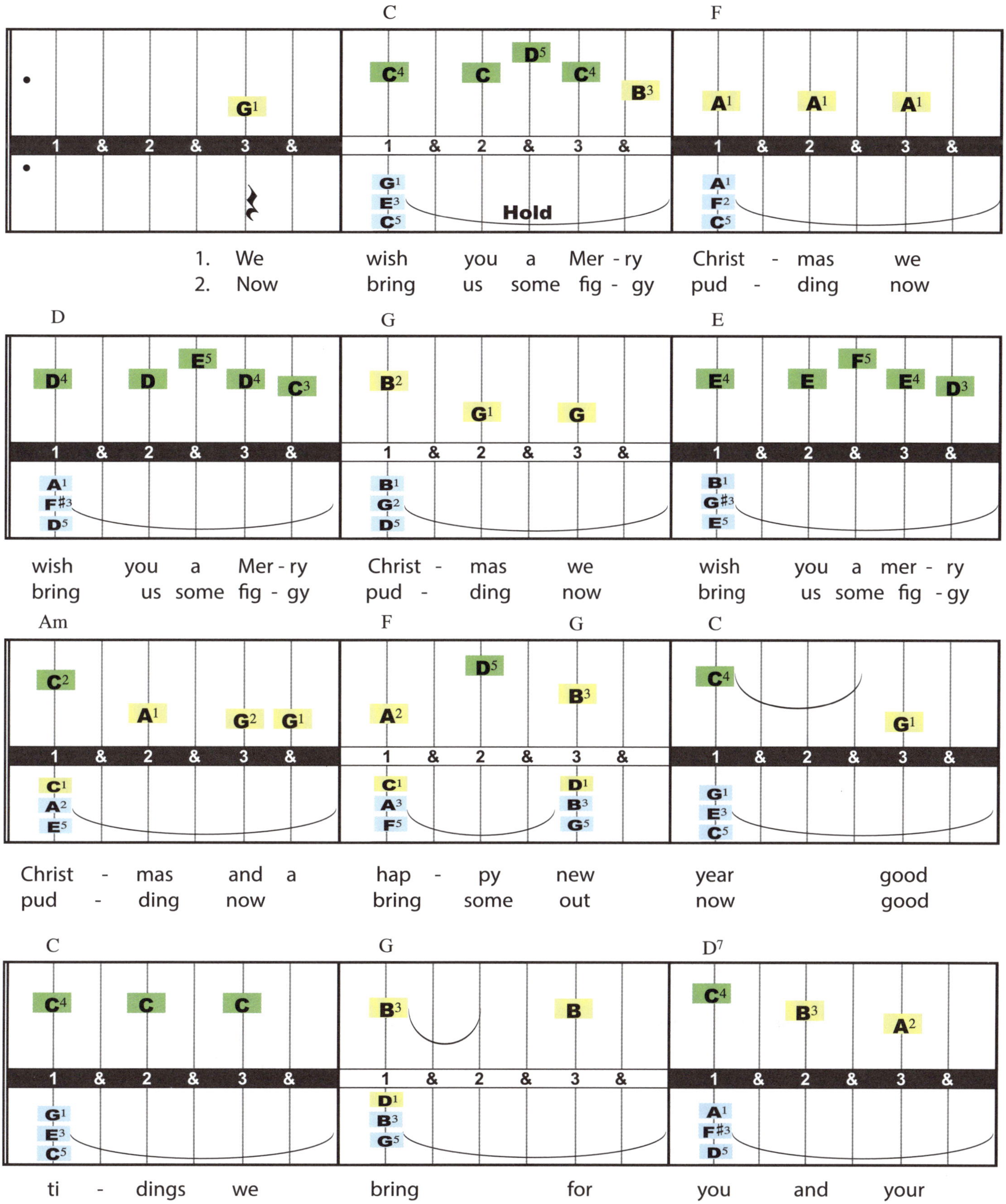

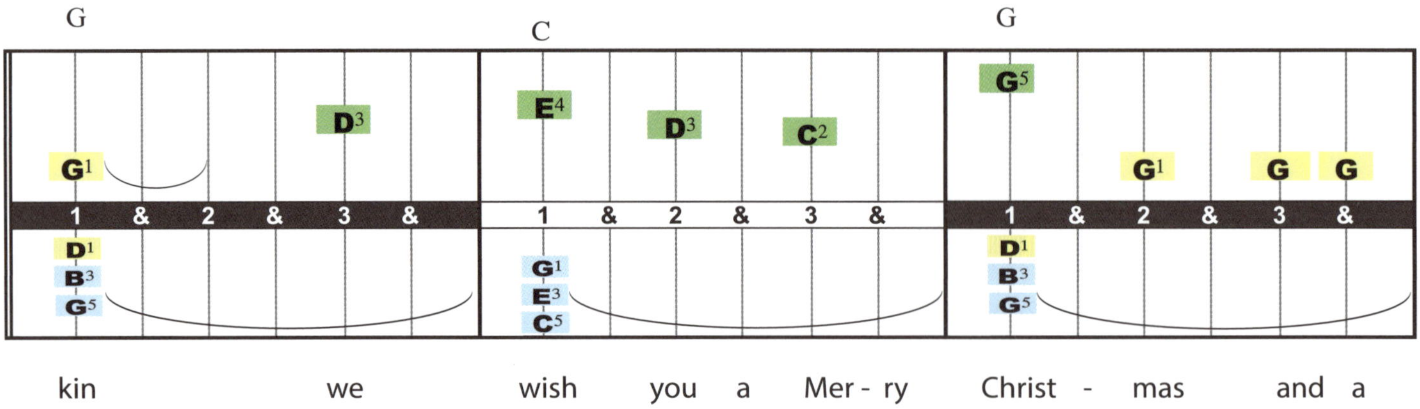

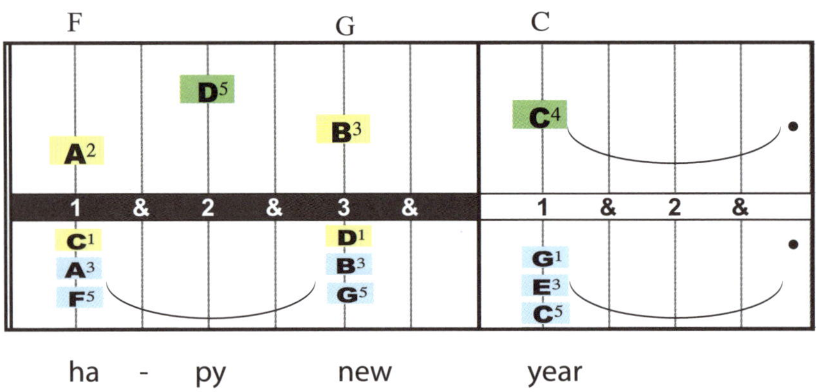

Verse 3
We wont go until we get some
We wont go until we get some
We wont go until we get some
So bring it right here

Verse 4
We all like our figgy pudding
We all like our figgy pudding
We all like our figgy pudding
with all its good cheers

Rudolph the Red-Nosed Reindeer

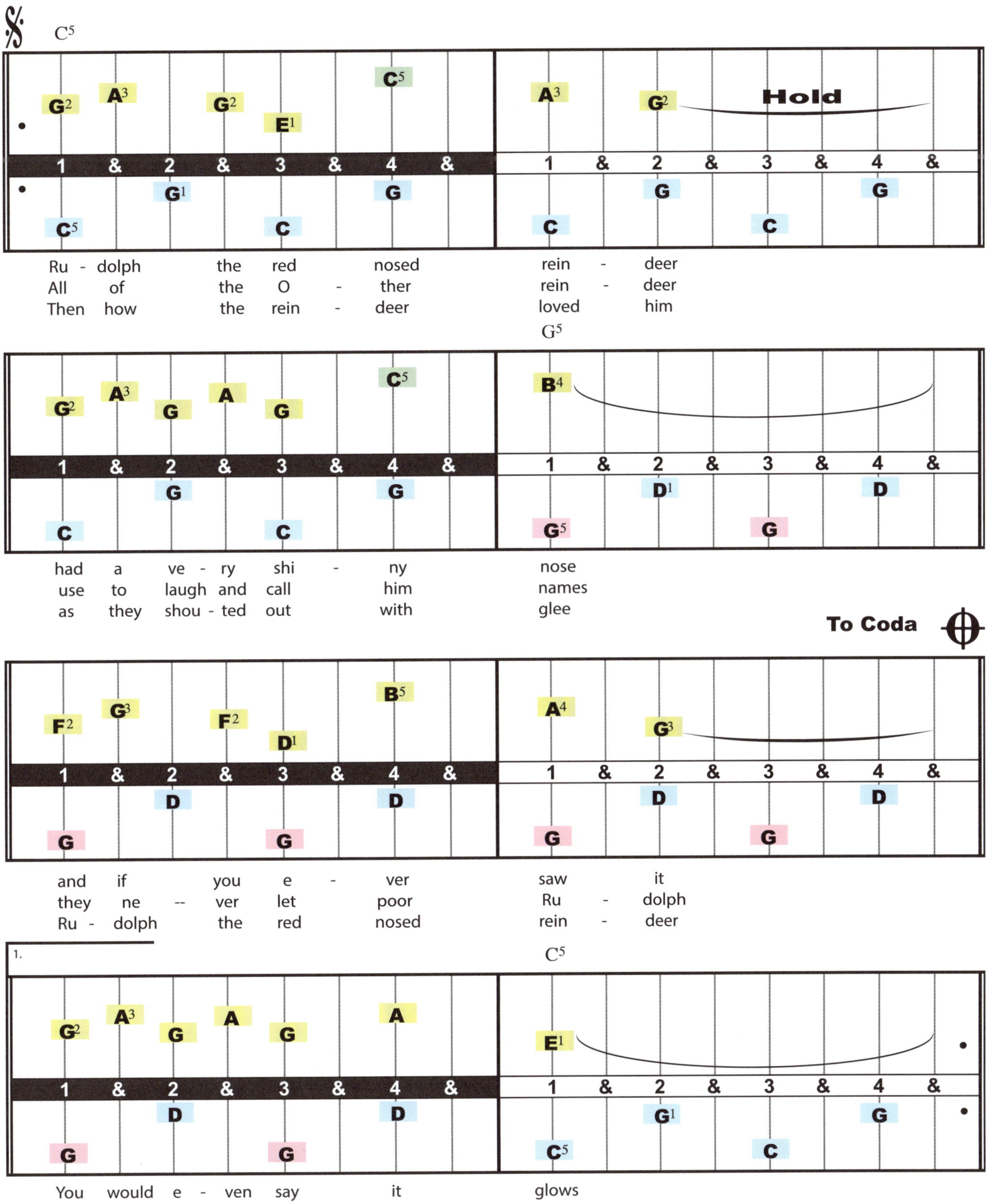

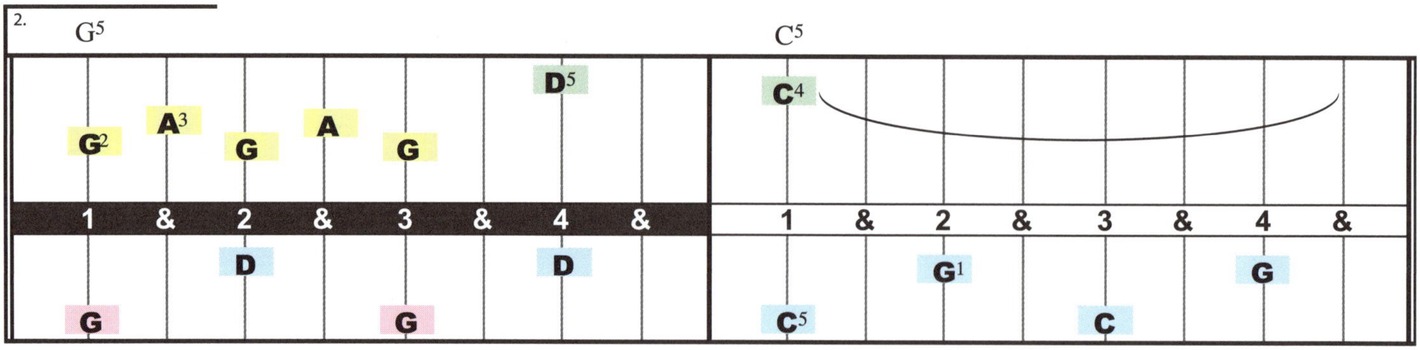

join in an - y rein - deer games

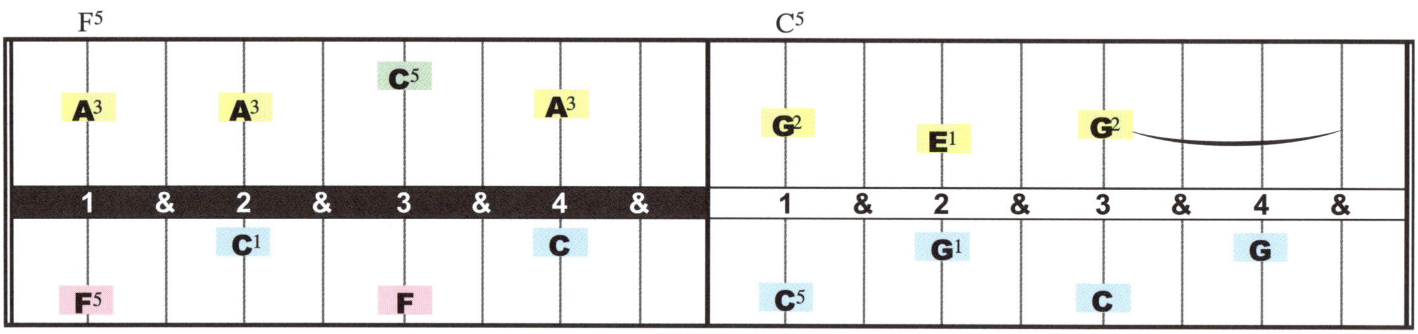

Then one fog - gy Christ - mas eve

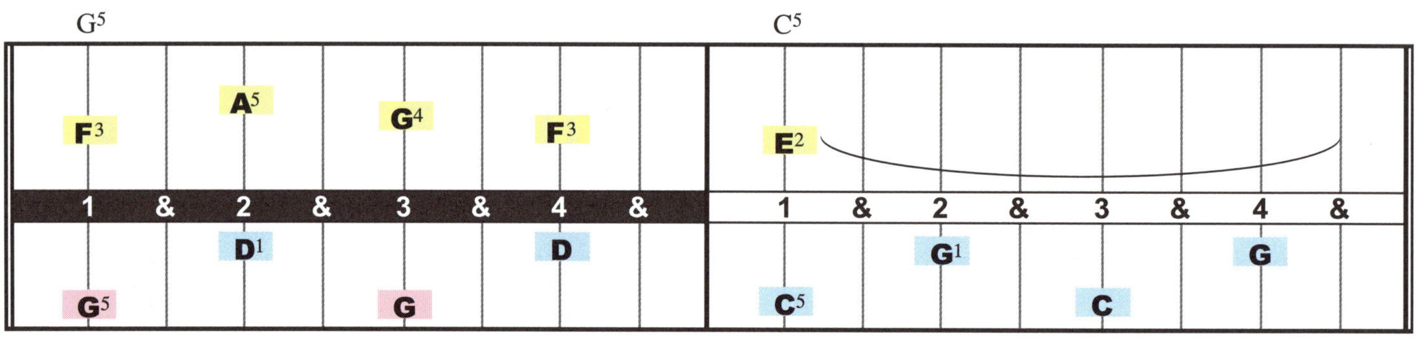

San - ta came to say

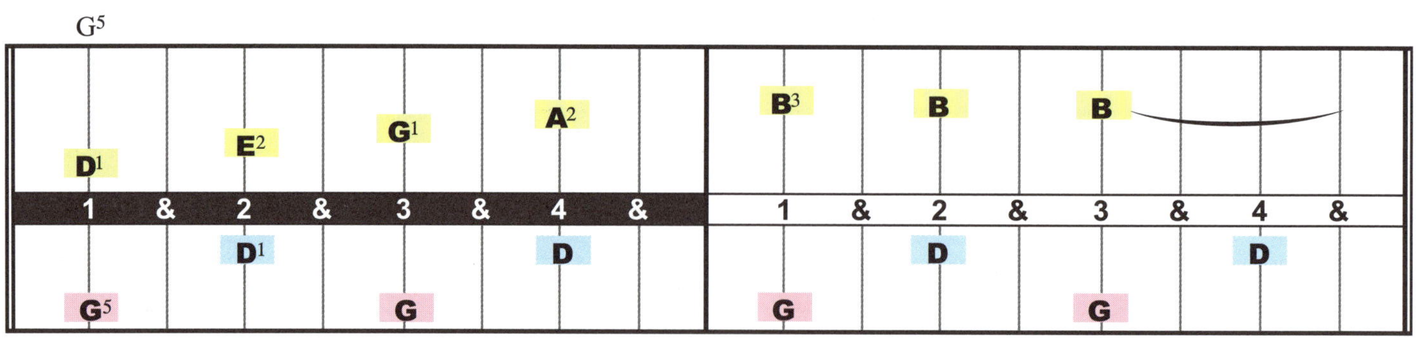

"Ru - dolph with your nose so bright

D.S. Al Coda

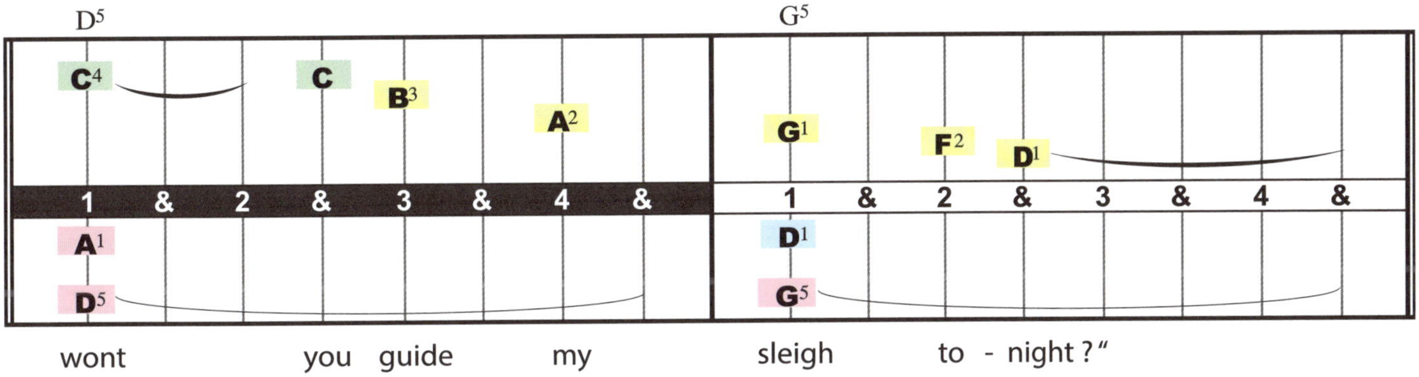

Coda

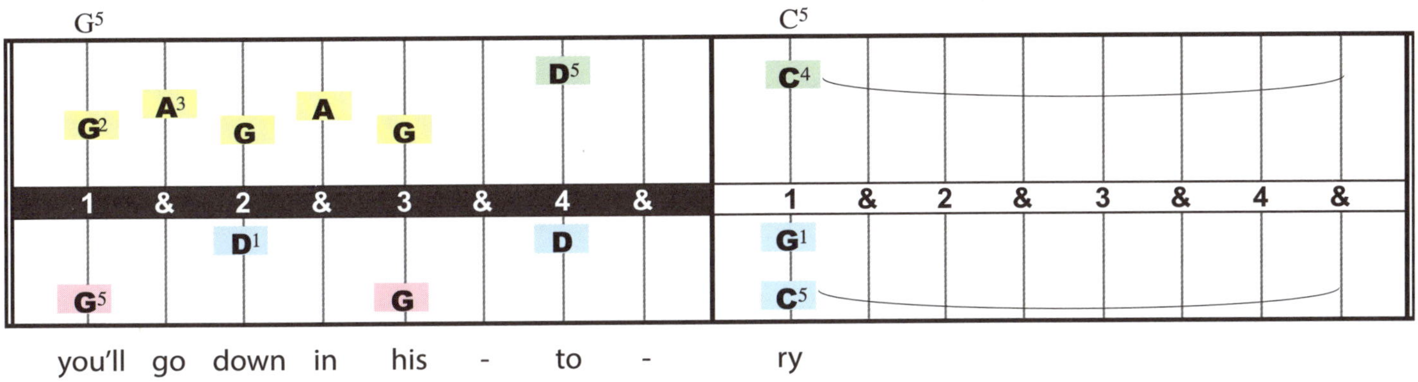

We Three Kings

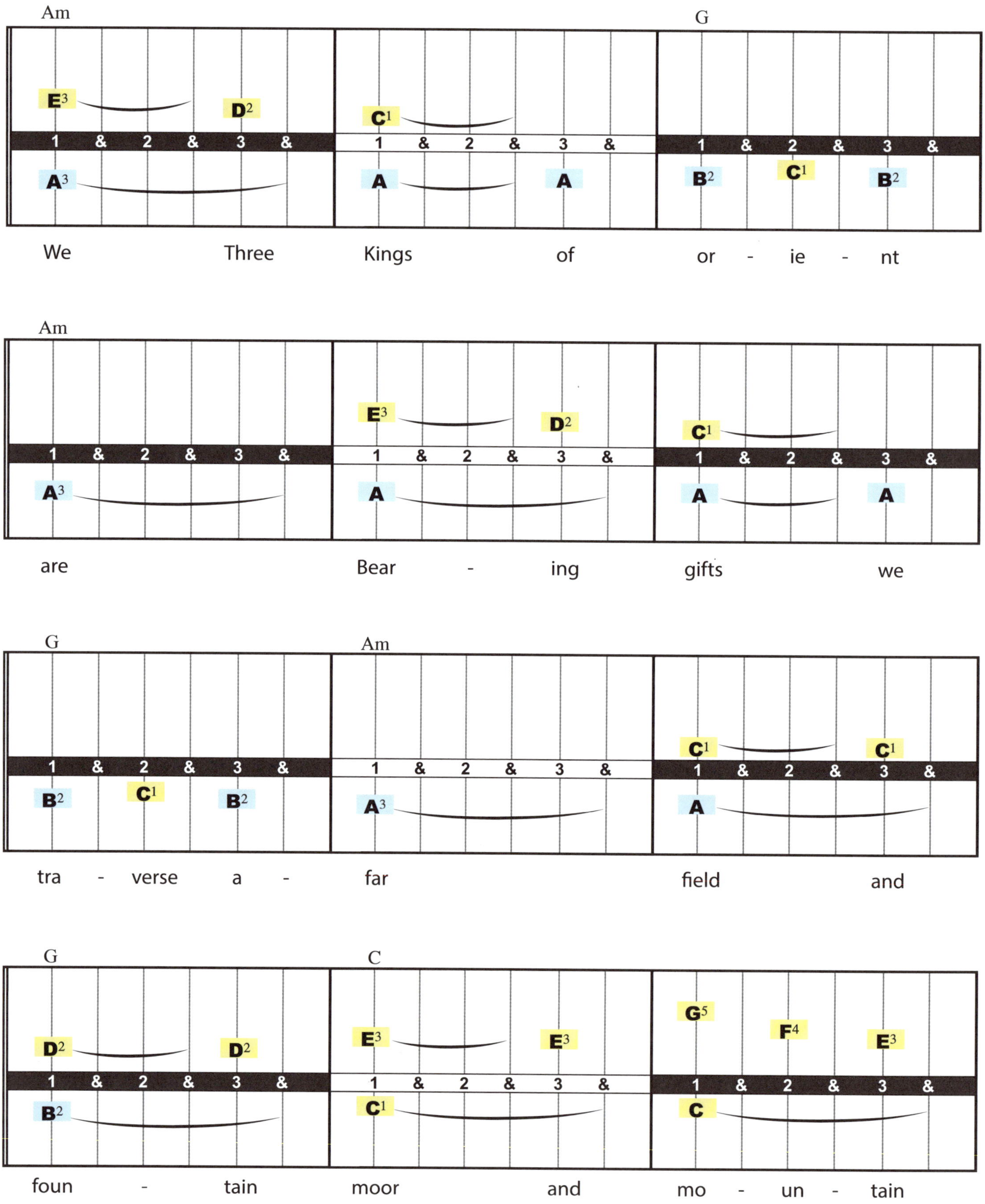

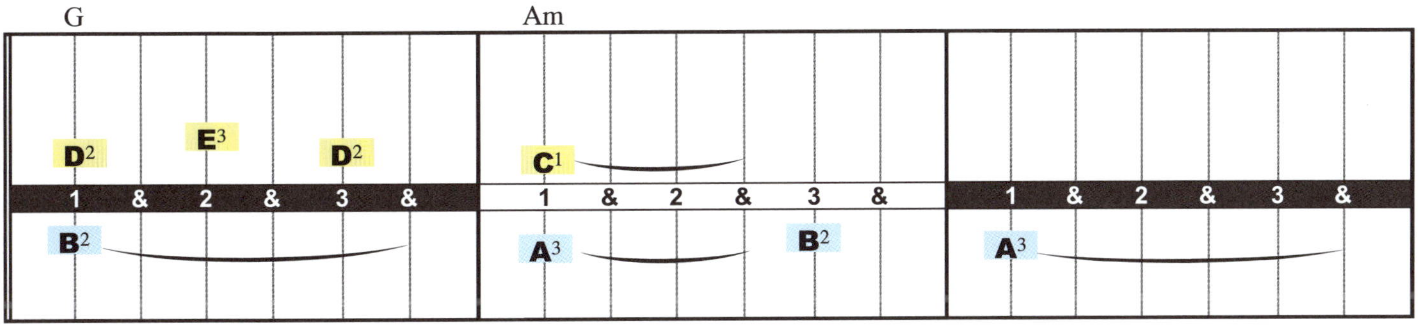

fol - low - ing yon - der star

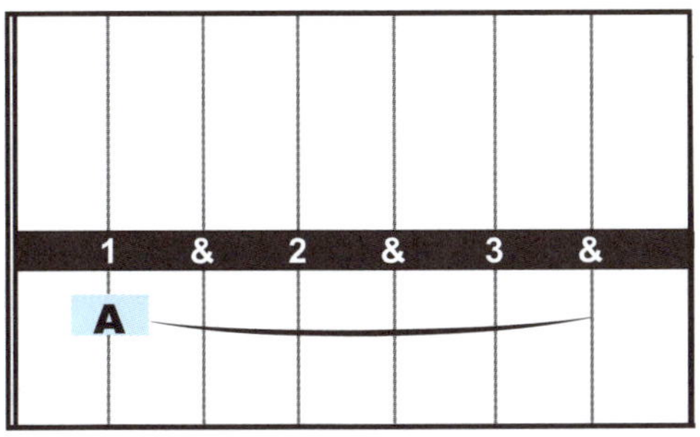

Verse 2
Born a King on Bethlehem's plain
Gold I bring to crown Him again
King for ever, ceasing never
Over us all to reign

Verse 3
Frankincense to offer have I
Incense owns a Deity nigh
Prayer and praising, all men raising worship
Him, God most high

Verse 4
Myrrh is mine Its bitter perfume
Breathes a life of gathering gloom
Sorrowing, sighing, bleeding, dying
Sealed in the stone cold tomb

Verse 5
Glorious now behold Him arise
King and God and Sacrifice!
Al-le-lu-ia, al-le-lu-ia
Heaven to earth replies

Verse 6
Then let us all rejoice again
On Christmas Day, on Christmas Day
Then let us all rejoice again
On Christmas Day in the morning

I Saw Three Ships

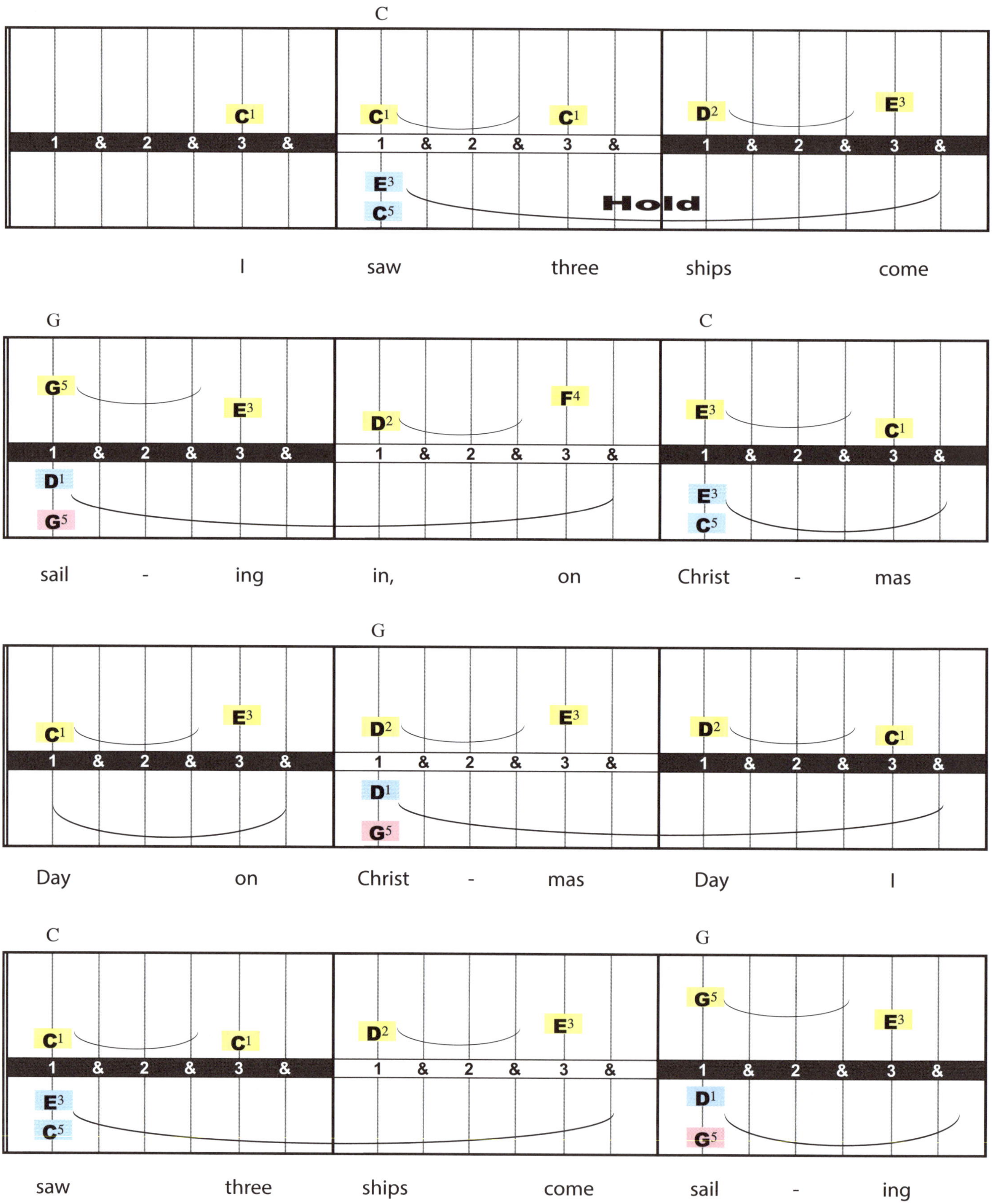

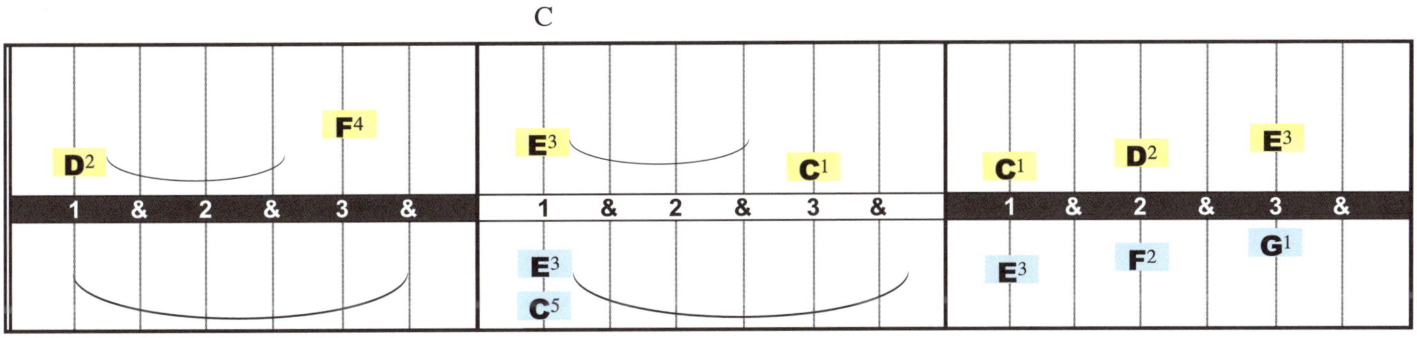

in, on Christ - mas Day in the

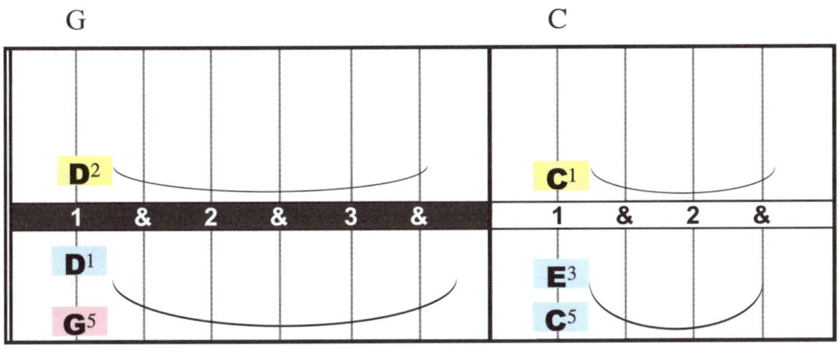

morn - ing

Verse 2
And what was in those ships all three
On Christmas Day, on Christmas Day?
And what was in those ships all three
On Christmas Day in the morning?

Verse 3
Frankincense to offer have I
Incense owns a Deity nigh
Prayer and praising, all men raising worship
Him, God most high

Verse 4
And all the bells on Earth shall ring
On Christmas Day, on Christmas Day
And all the bells on Earth shall ring
On Christmas Day in the morning

Verse 5
And all the angels in Heaven shall sing
On Christmas Day, on Christmas Day
And all the angels in Heaven shall sing
On Christmas Day in the morning

Verse 6
Then let us all rejoice again
On Christmas Day, on Christmas Day
Then let us all rejoice again
On Christmas Day in the morning

Frosty The Snow Man

Verse

C

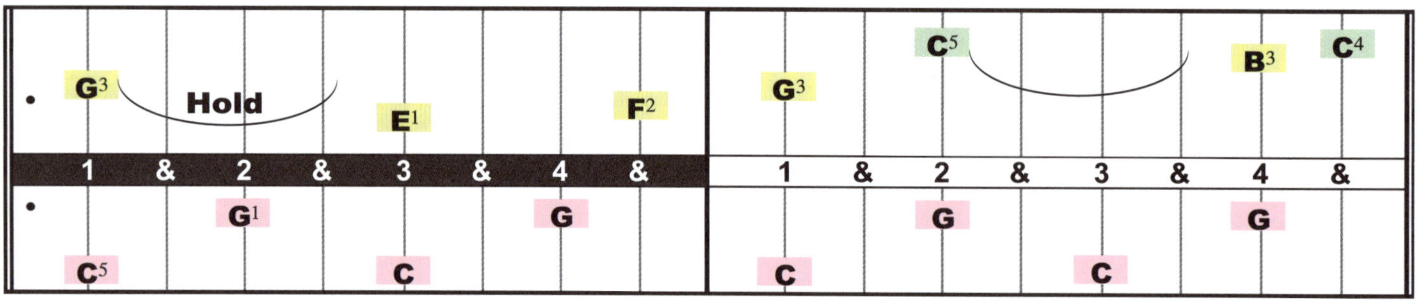

1. Fros - ty the snow man was a
2. Fros - ty the snow man is a

F C

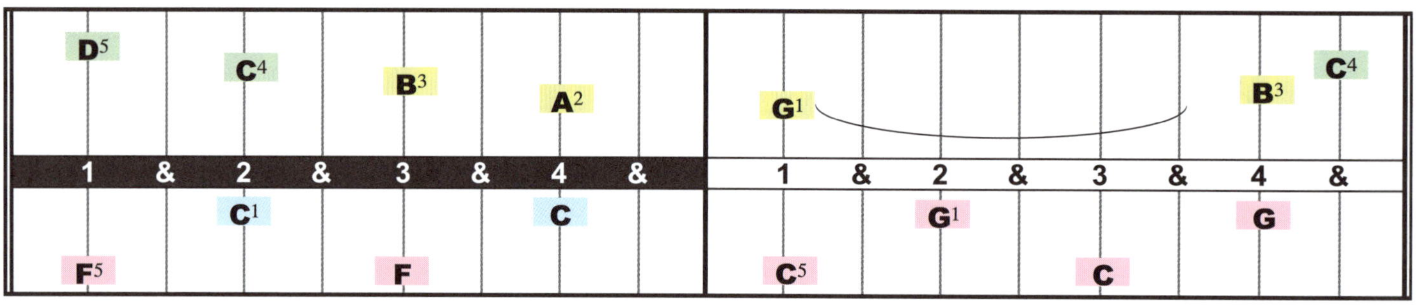

jol - ly hap - py soul with a
fai - ry tail they say he was

F C

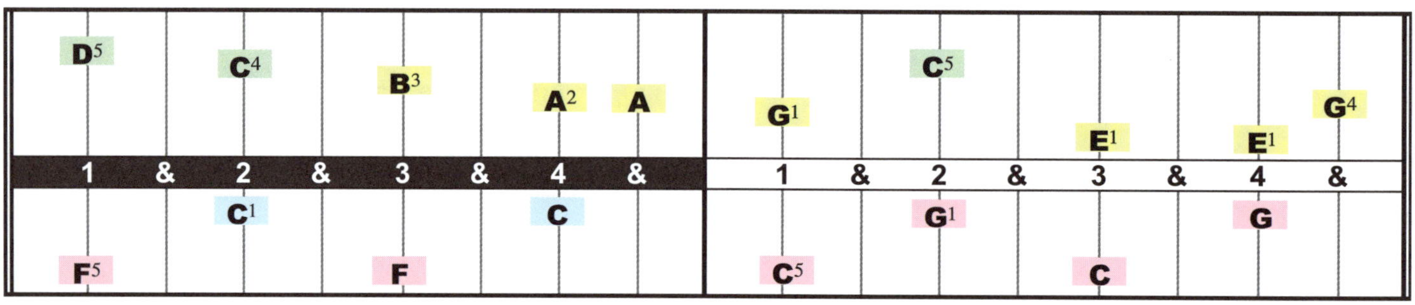

corn cob pipe and a but - ton nose and two
made of snow but the Chil - dren know how he

1. 4. G C

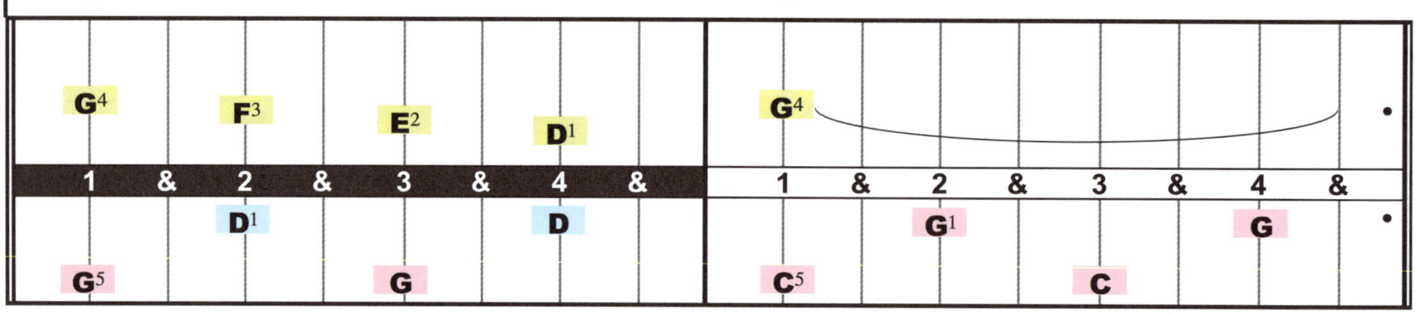

eyes made out of coal

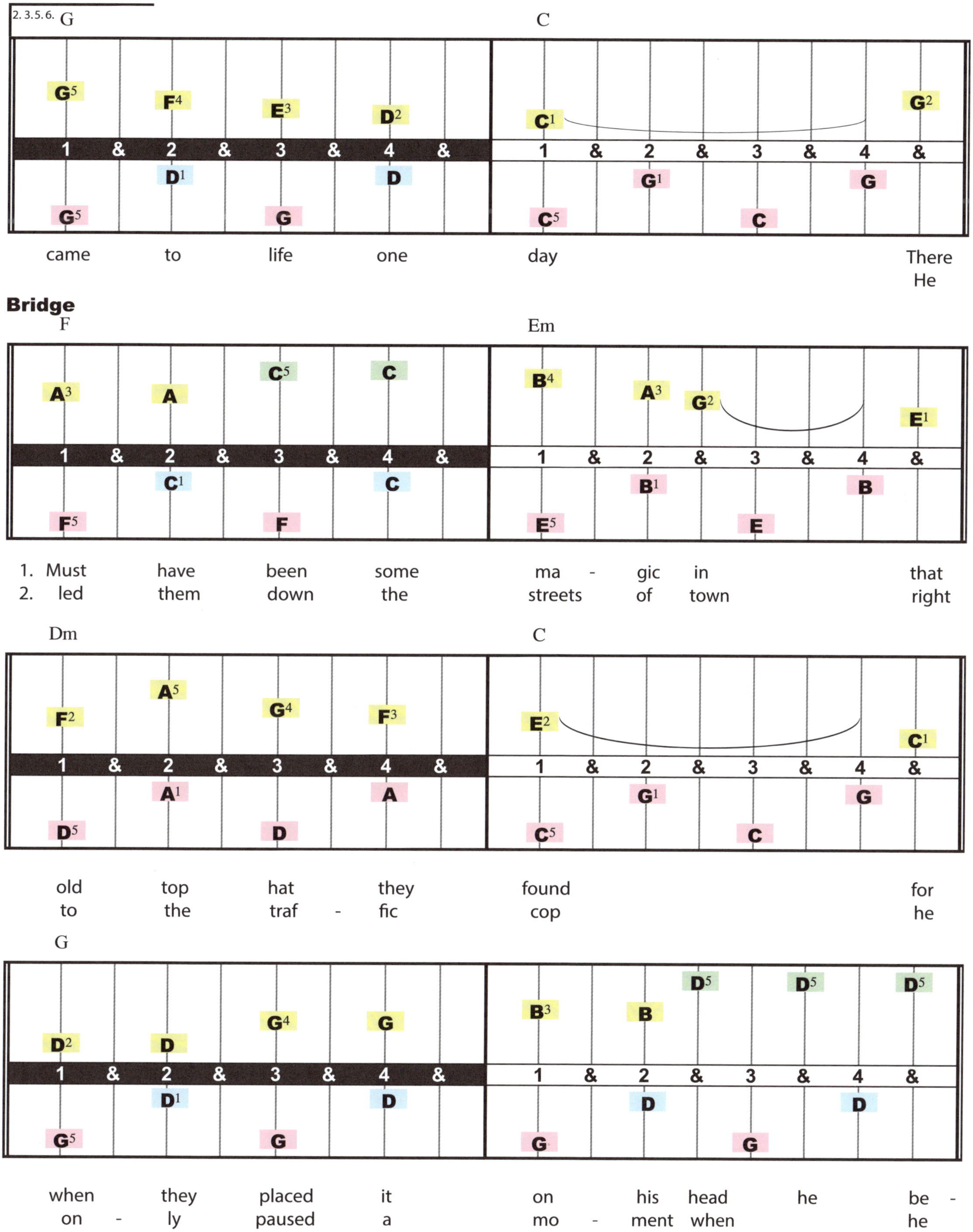
2. 3. 5. 6. G
C
came to life one day There
He
Bridge
F
Em
1. Must have been some ma - gic in that
2. led them down the streets of town right
Dm
C
old top hat they found for
to the traf - fic cop he
G
when they placed it on his head he be -
on - ly paused a mo - ment when he

D

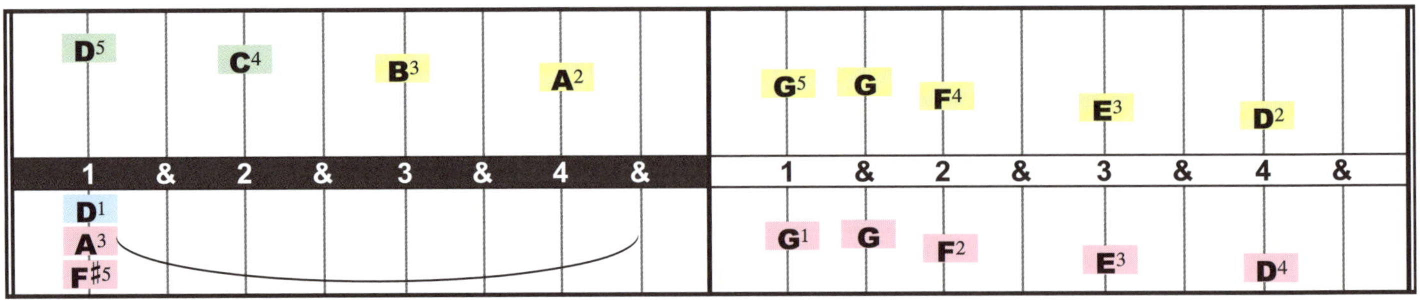

- gan to dance a - round oh
heard him holl - ar "stop!" oh

Chorus

C

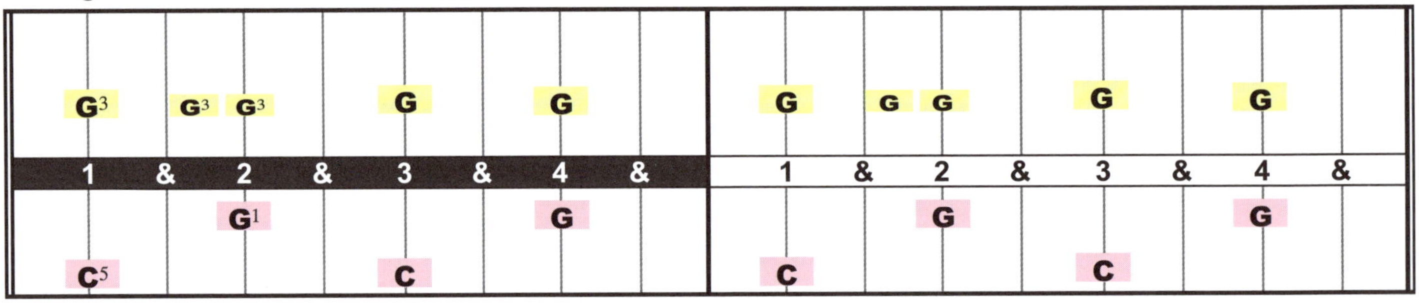

Thum - pe - ty Thump Thump Thum - pe - ty Thump Thump

G

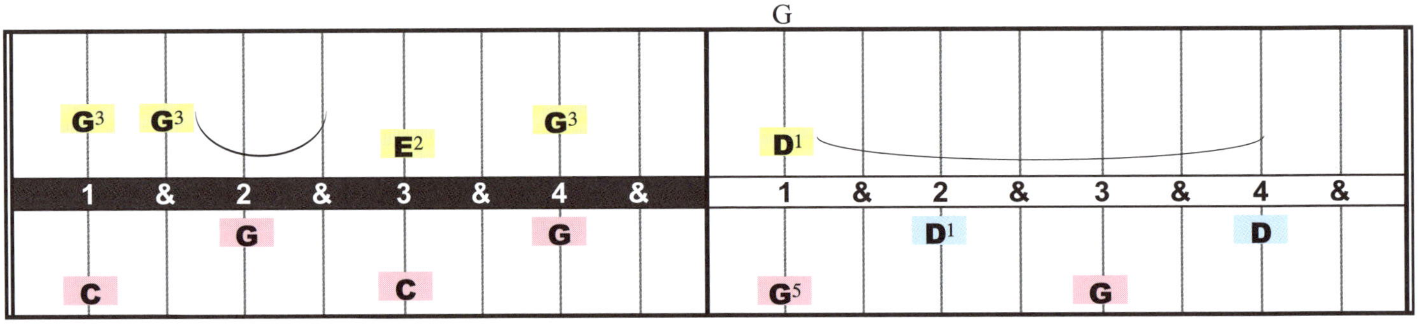

Look at Fros - ty go

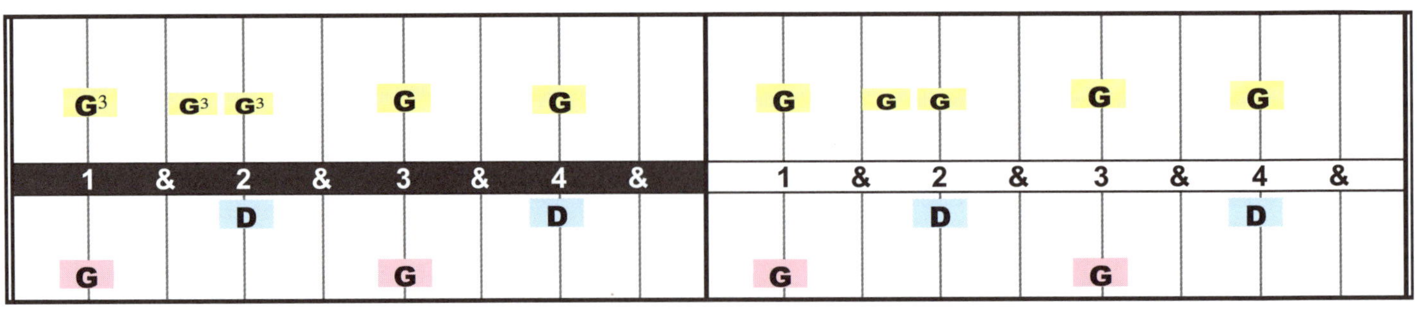

Thum - pe - ty Thump Thump Thum - pe - ty Thump Thump

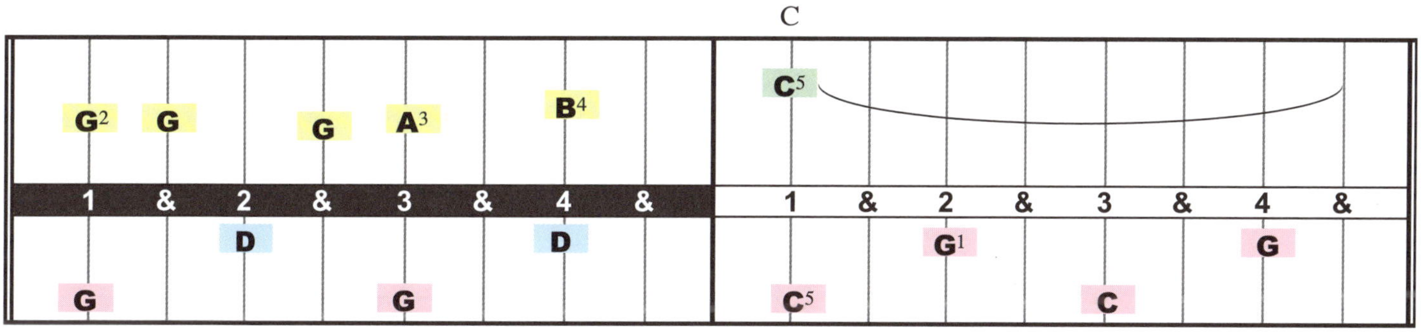

Ov - er the hills of snow

Structure

Verse - Verse - Bridge - Verse - Chorus - Verse - Verse - Bridge - Verse

Verse 3
Frosty the snowman, was alive
As he could be and the
Children say he could laugh
And play just the same as you and me

Verse 4
Oh Frosty the snowman knew
The sun was hot that day. So
He said, "Let's run and we'll
Have some fun now before I melt away!"

Verse 5
Down to the village with a
Broomstick in his hand. Running
Here and there all around the
Square saying "Catch me if you can!"

Verse 6
Oh, Frosty the snowman had to
Hurry on his way. But he waved
Goodbye, saying "Don't you cry, I'll
Be back again someday."

Deck the Halls

Verse A

C

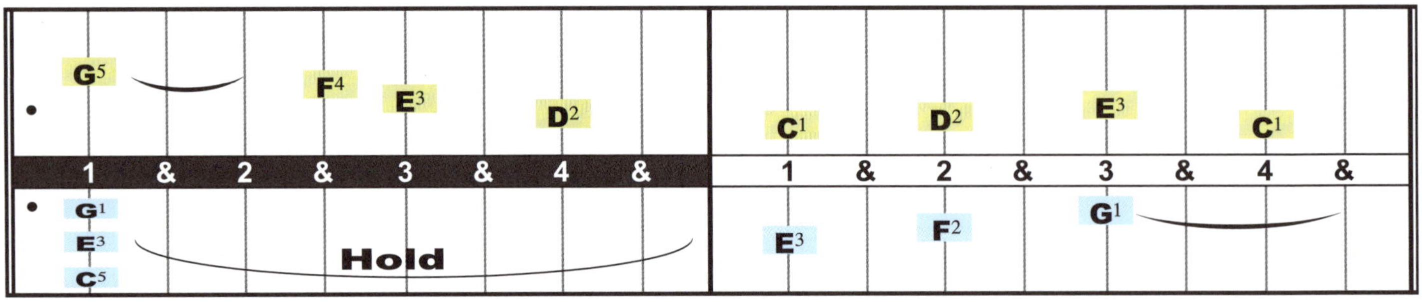

Deck the halls with boughs of hol - ly
Tis the sea - son to be jol - ly

GI C G C

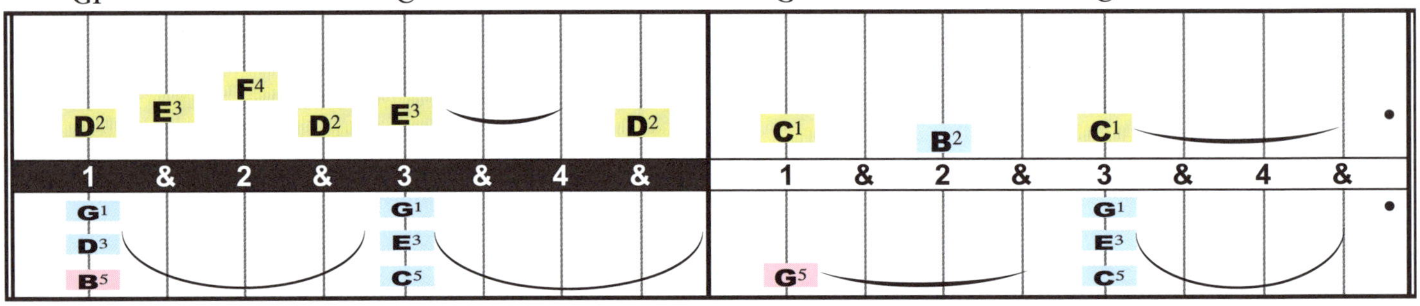

Fa la la la la la la la la
Fa la la la la la la la la

Bridge

GI C

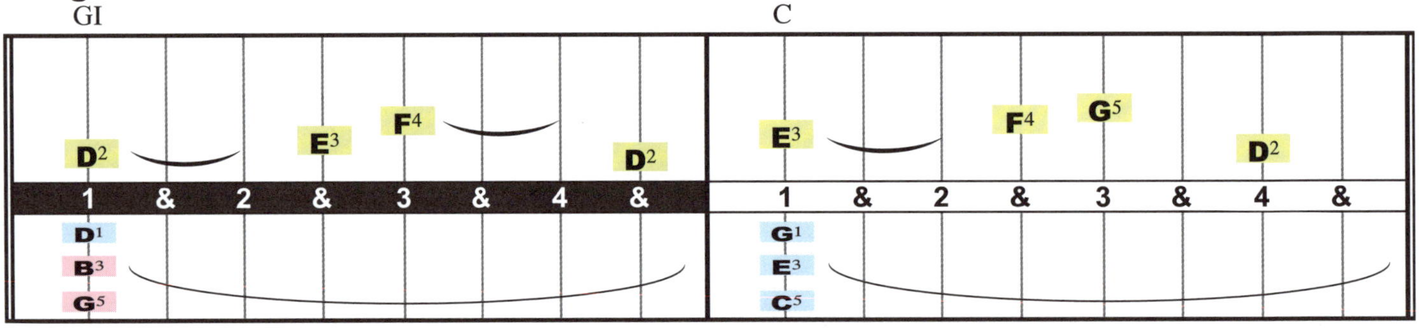

Don we now our gay ap - par - el

C FII GI

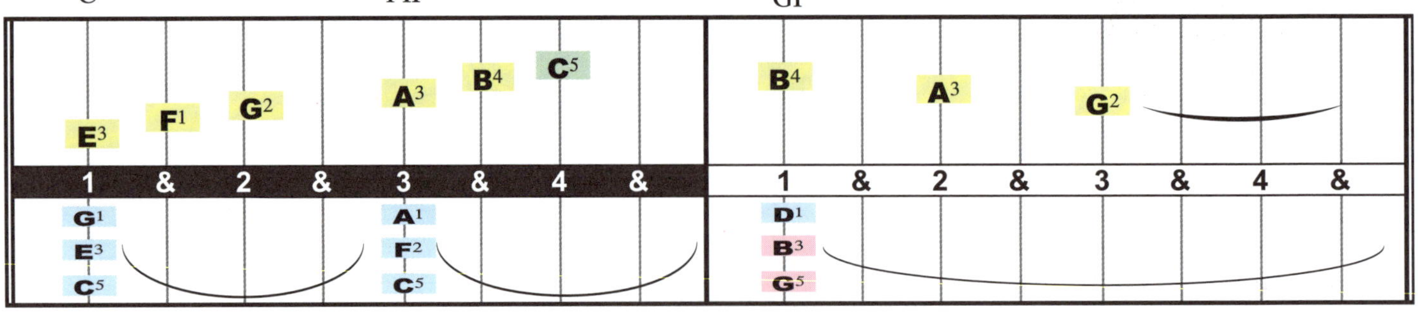

Fa la la la la la la la la

Verse B

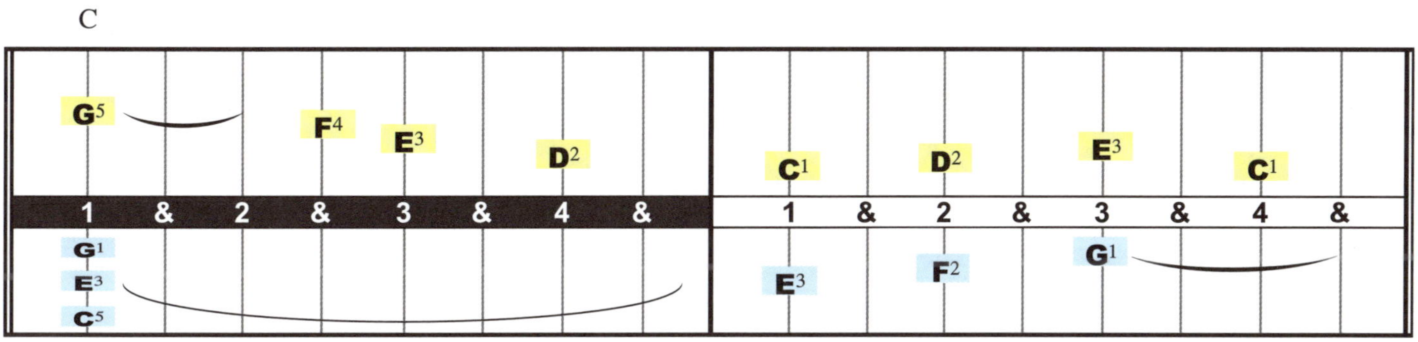

Troll the an - cient yule tide car - ol

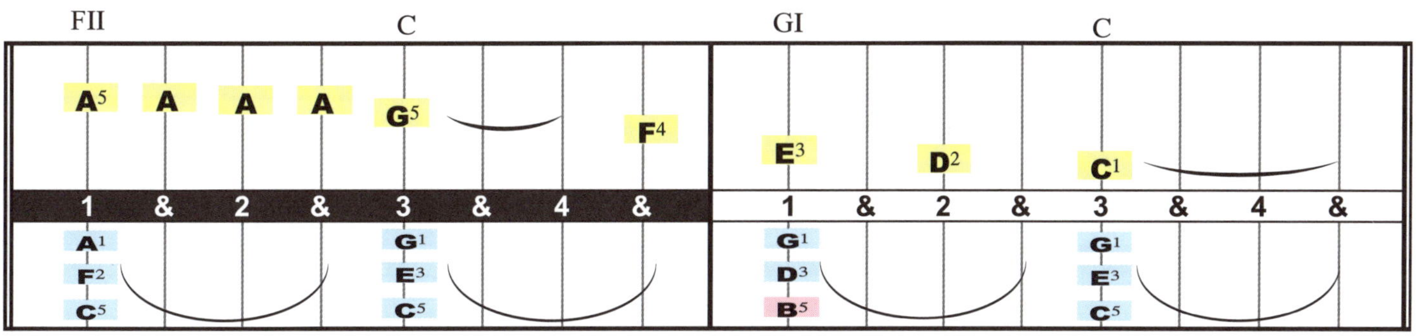

Fa la la la la la la la la

Structure

Verse A - Bridge - Verse B

Verse 2A
See the blazing yule before us
Fa la la la la, la la la la
Strike the harp and join the chorus
Fa la la la la, la la la la

Bridge 2
Follow me in merry measure
Fa la la la la la la la la

Verse 2B
While I tell of Yule tide treasure
Fa la la la la la la la la

Verse 3A
Fast away the old year passes
Fa la la la la, la la la la
Hail the new ye lads and lasses
Fa la la la la, la la la la

Bridge 3
Sing we joy us, all together
Fa la la la la la la la la

Verse 3B
Headless of the wind and winter
Fa la la la la la la la la

Christmas Canon

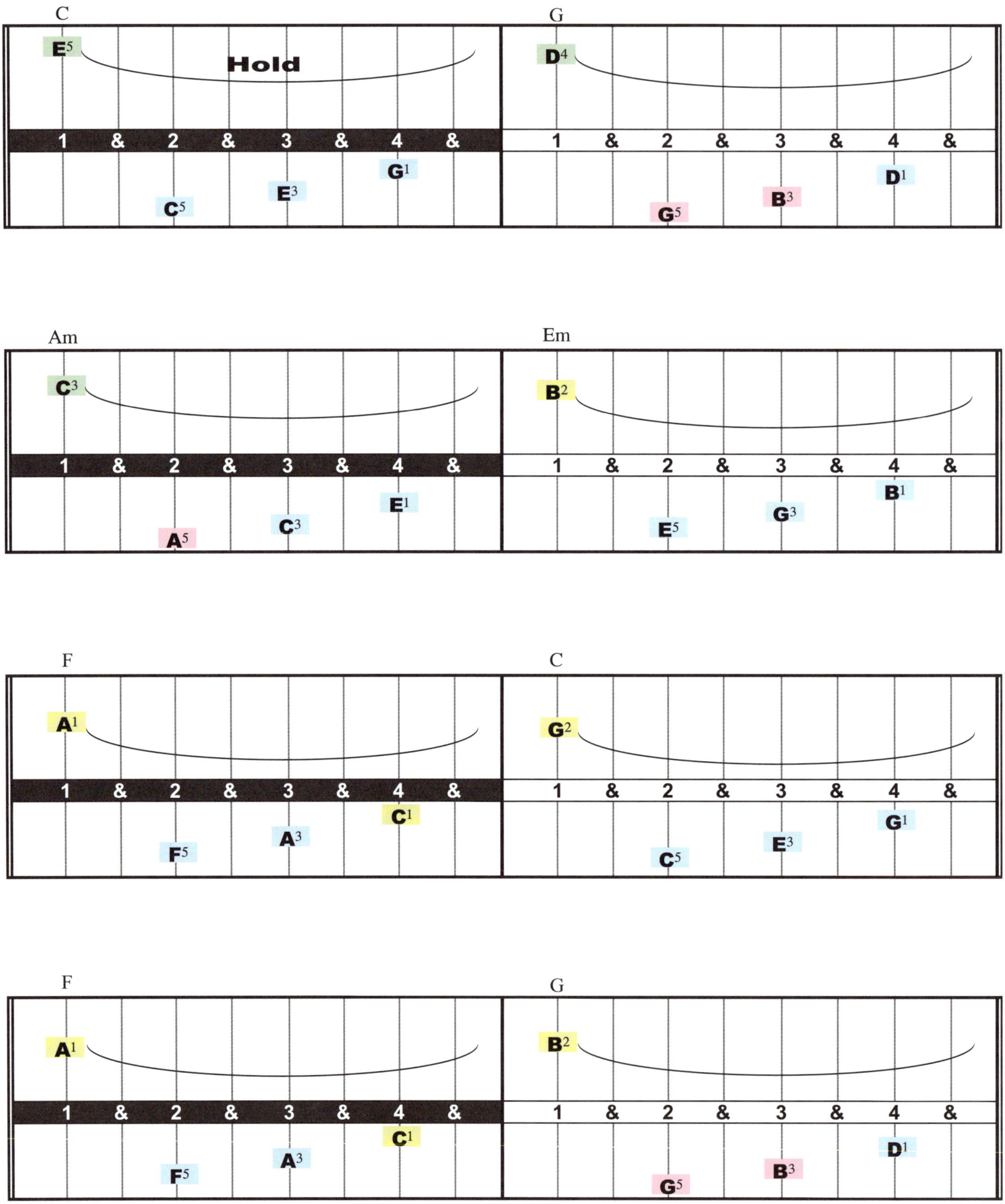

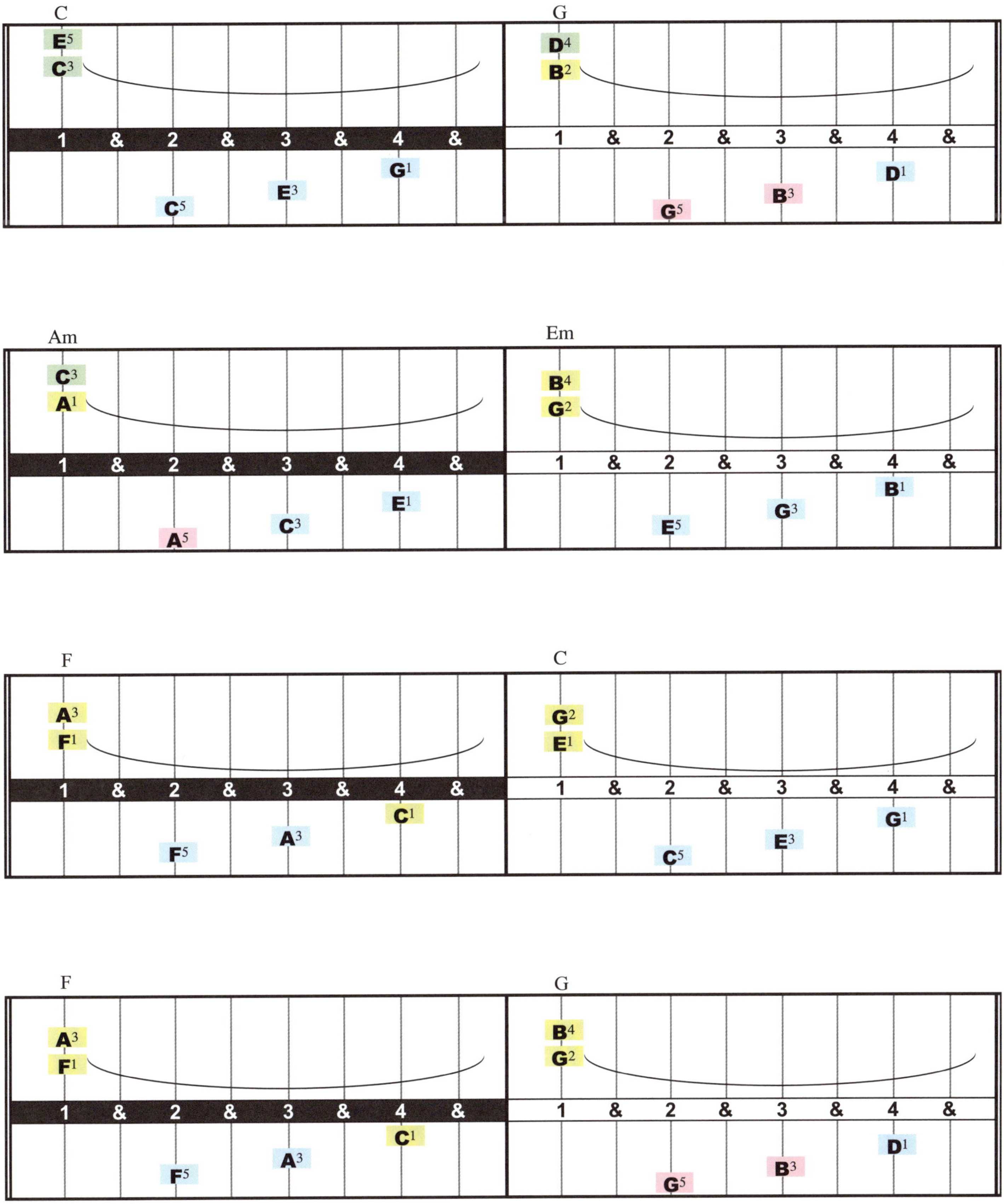
C
E5
C3
1 & 2 & 3 & 4 &
C5 E3 G1
G
D4
B2
1 & 2 & 3 & 4 &
G5 B3 D1
Am
C3
A1
1 & 2 & 3 & 4 &
A5 C3 E1
Em
B4
G2
1 & 2 & 3 & 4 &
E5 G3 B1
F
A3
F1
1 & 2 & 3 & 4 &
F5 A3 C1
C
G2
E1
1 & 2 & 3 & 4 &
C5 E3 G1
F
A3
F1
1 & 2 & 3 & 4 &
F5 A3 C1
G
B4
G2
1 & 2 & 3 & 4 &
G5 B3 D1

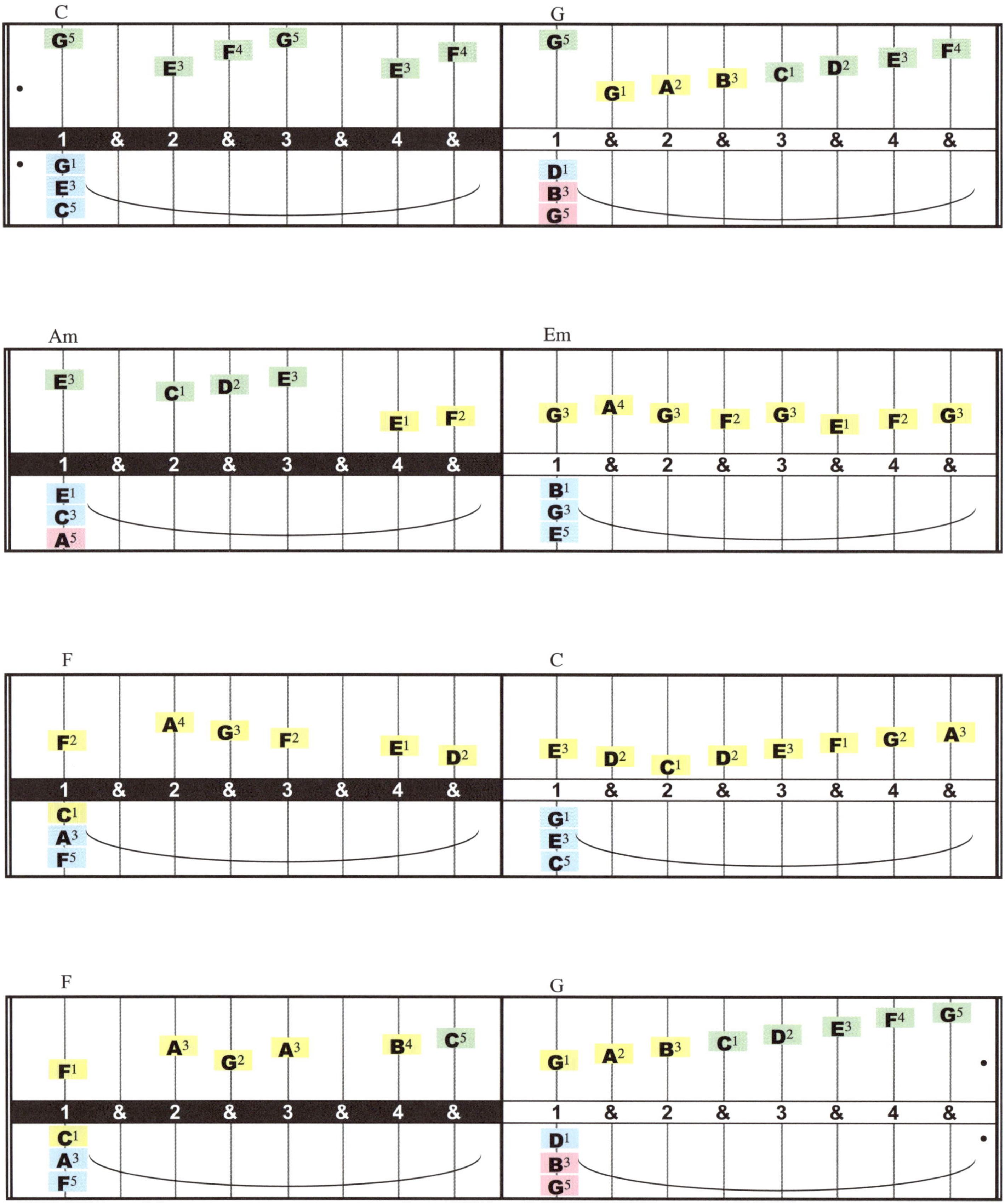
C
G
Am
Em
F
C
F
G

Joy to the World

Verse

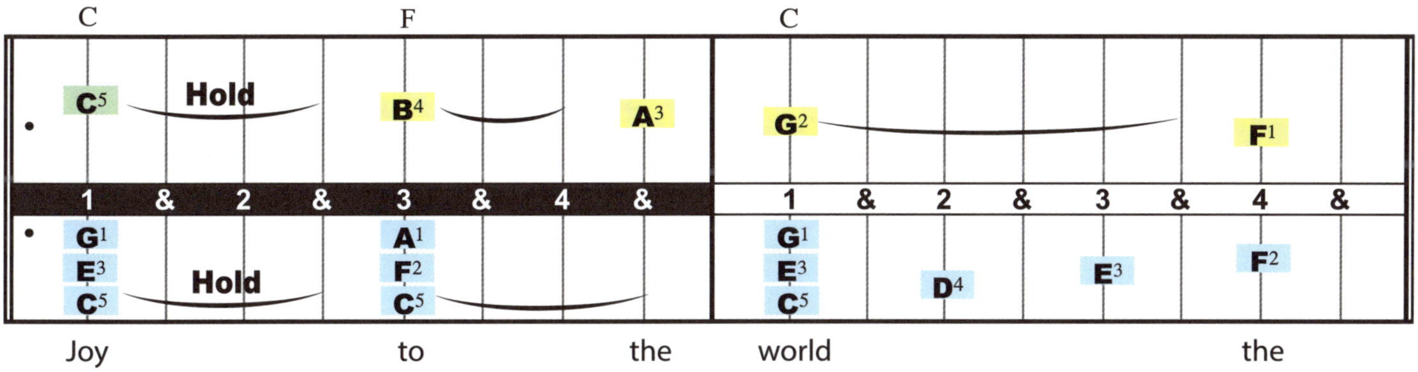

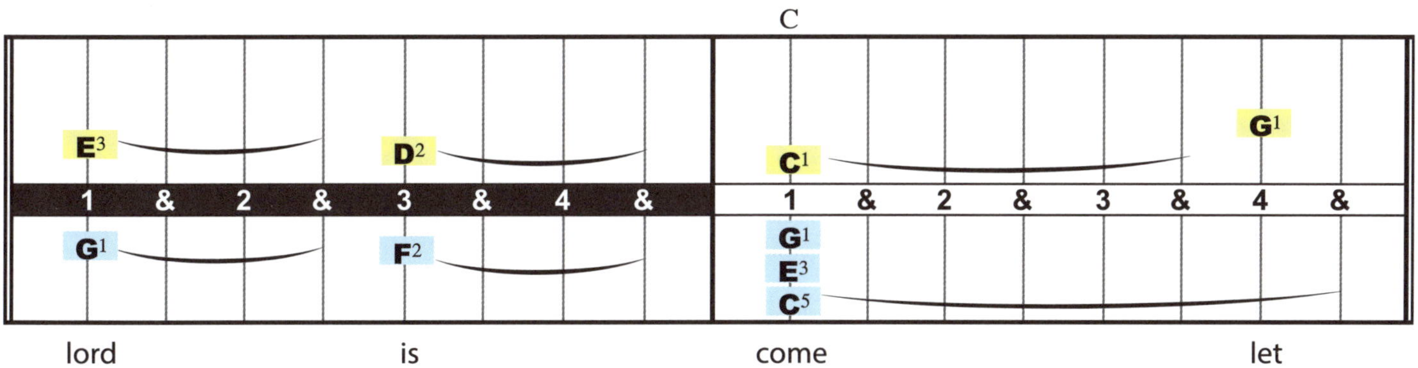

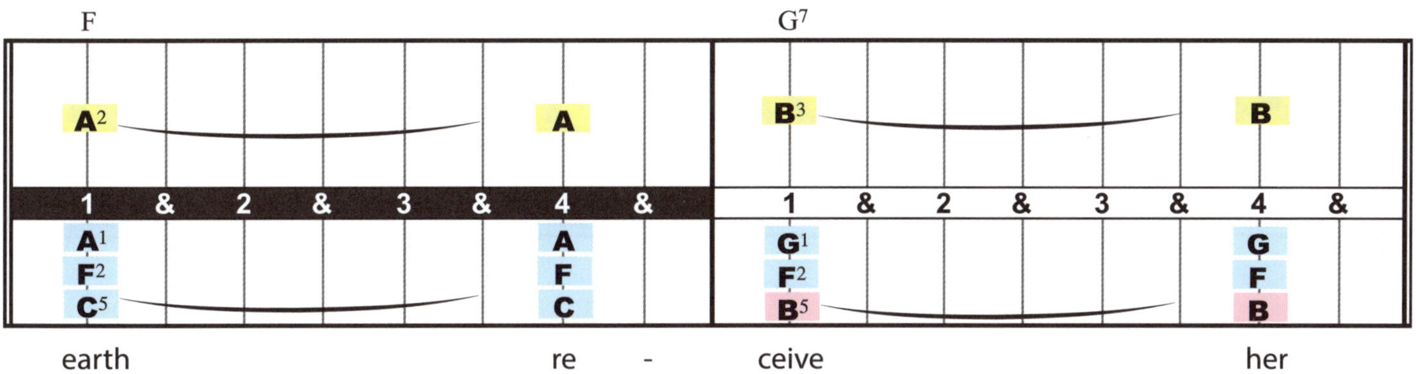

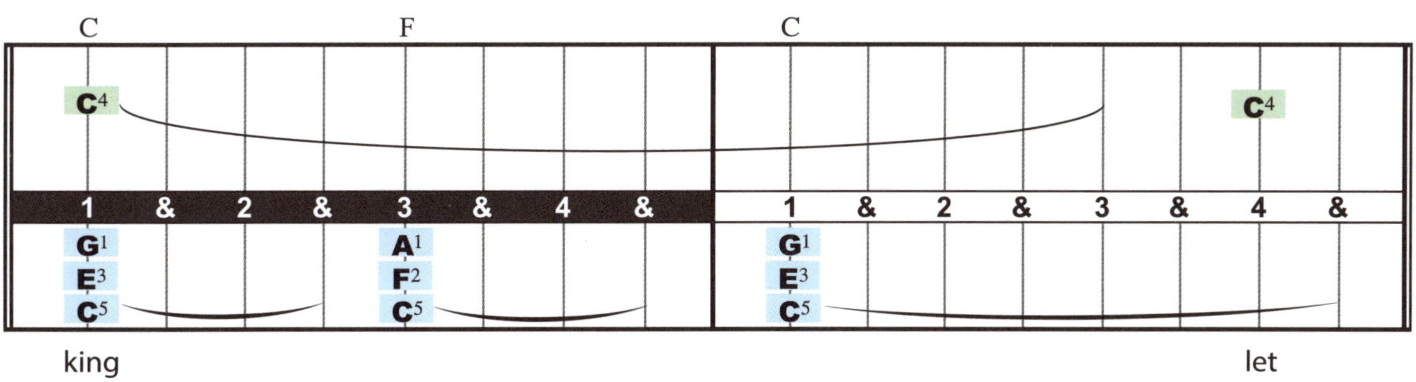

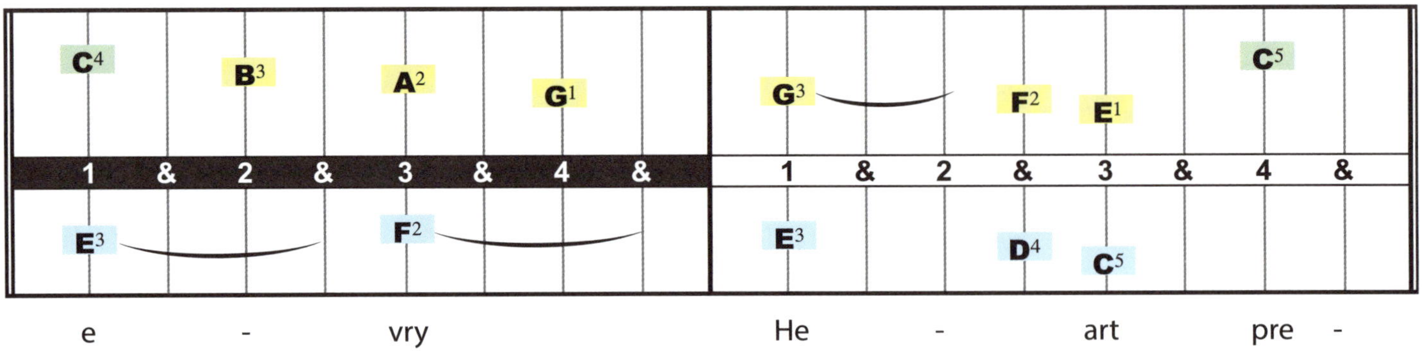
e - vry He - art pre -

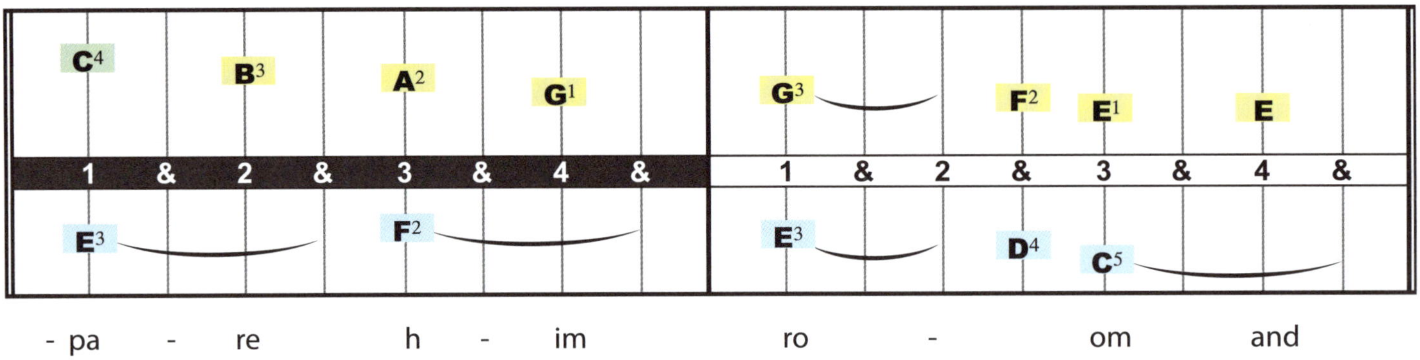
- pa - re h - im ro - om and

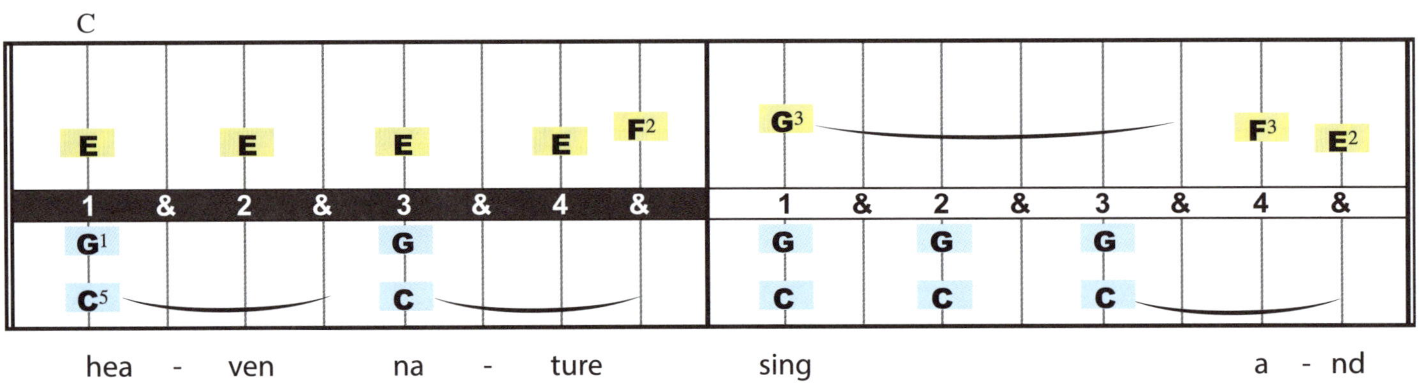
C
hea - ven na - ture sing a - nd

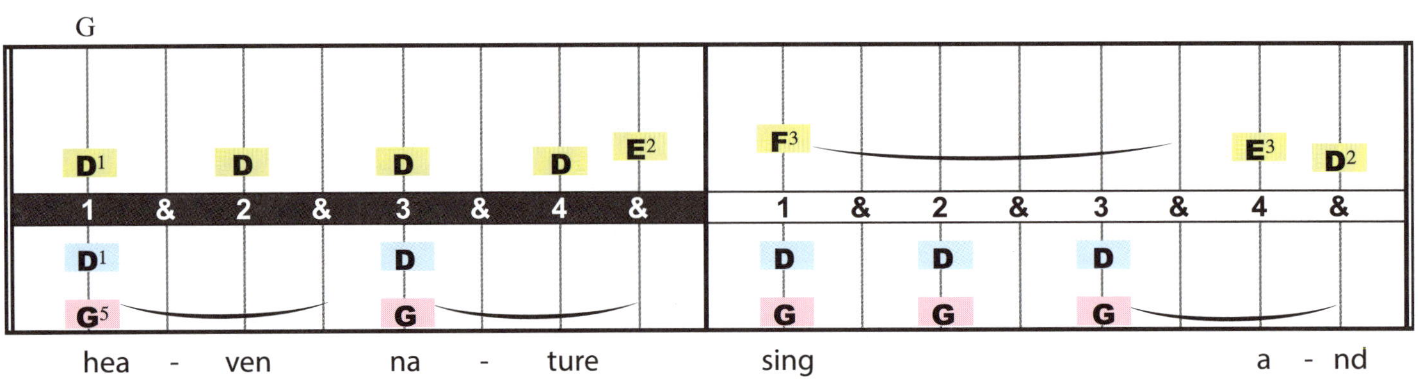
G
hea - ven na - ture sing a - nd

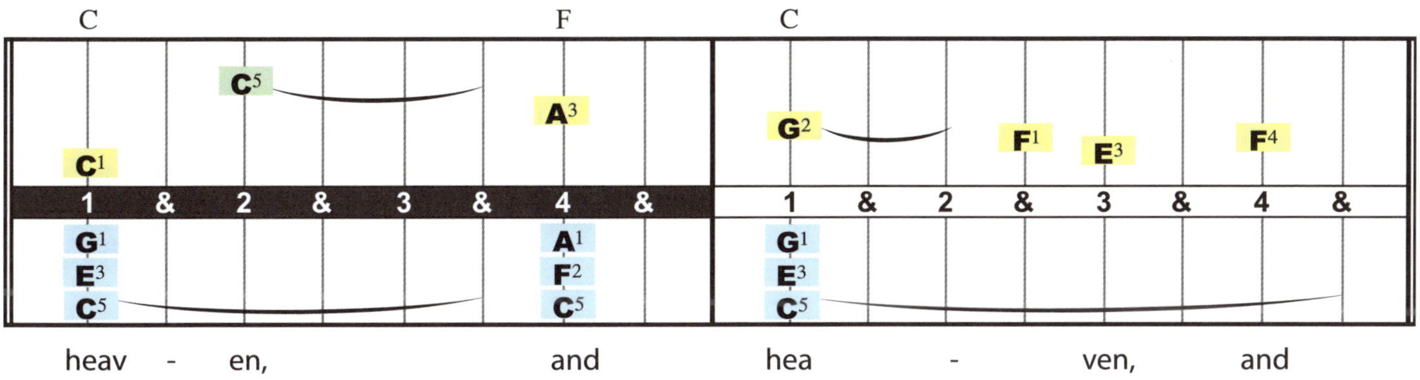

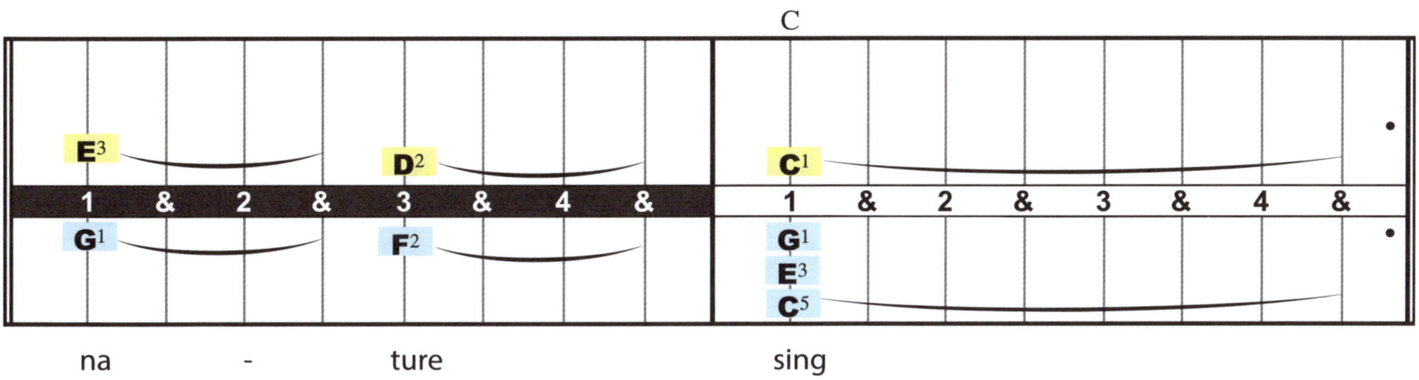

Verse 2

Joy to the world! The Saviour reigns;
Let men their songs employ;
While fields and floods, rocks, hills, and plains
Repeat the sounding joy,
Repeat the sounding joy,
Repeat, repeat the sounding joy.

Verse 3

He rules the world with truth and grace,
And makes the nations prove
The glories of His righteousness,
And wonders of His love,
And wonders of His love,
And wonders, wonders, of His love.

Carol of the Bells

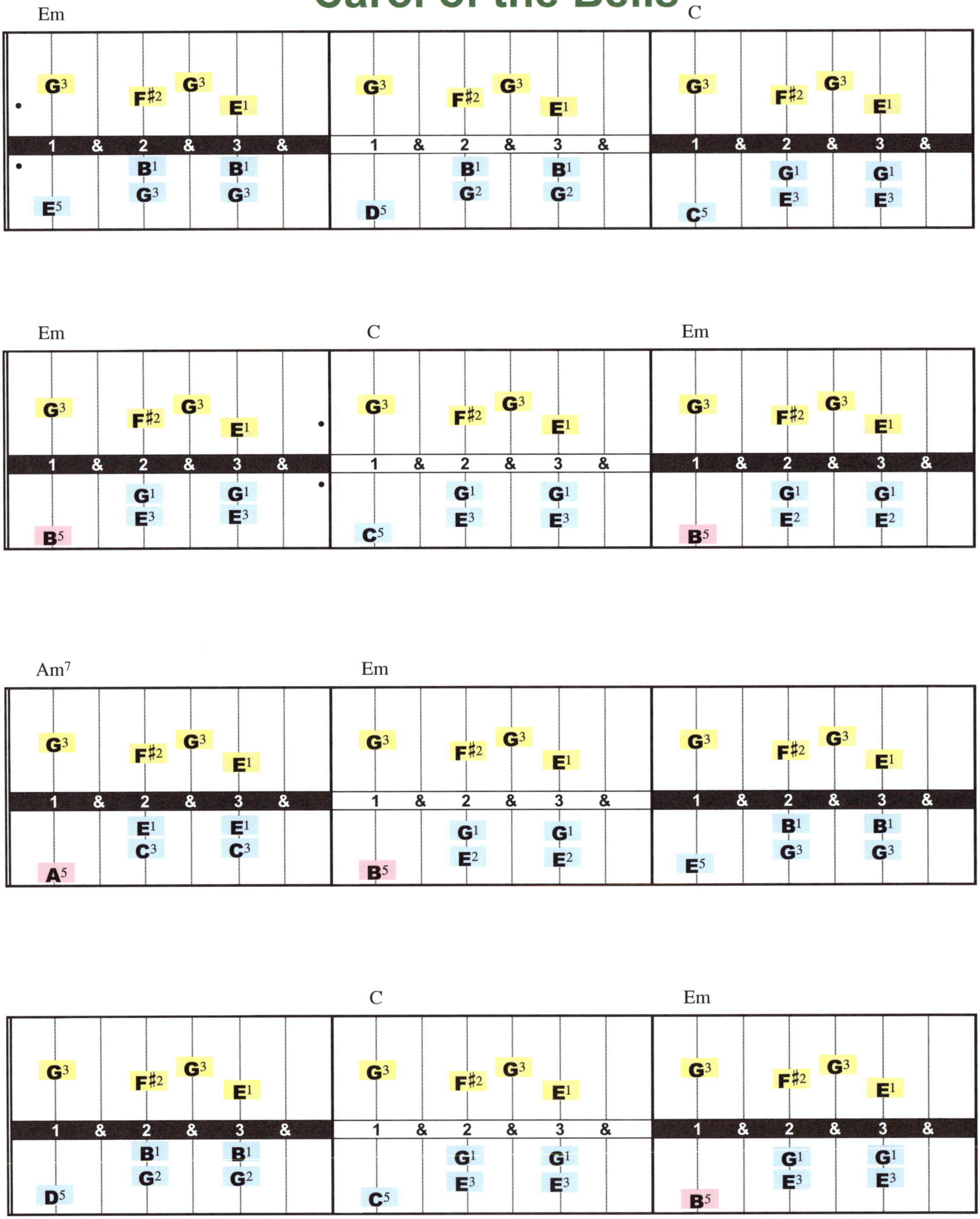

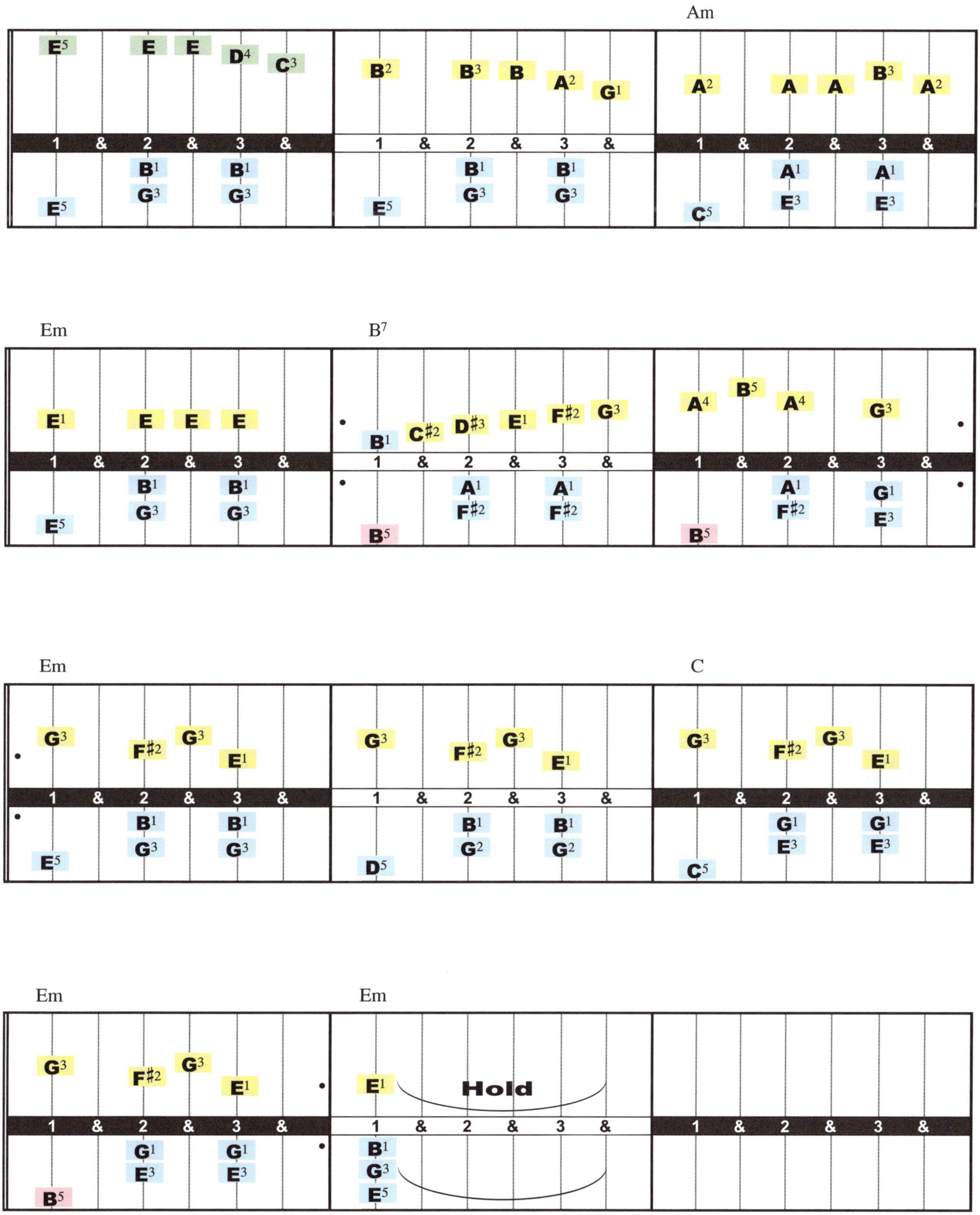
Am
Em
B7
Em
C
Em
Em
Hold
1 & 2 & 3 &

Silent Night - Sing Along

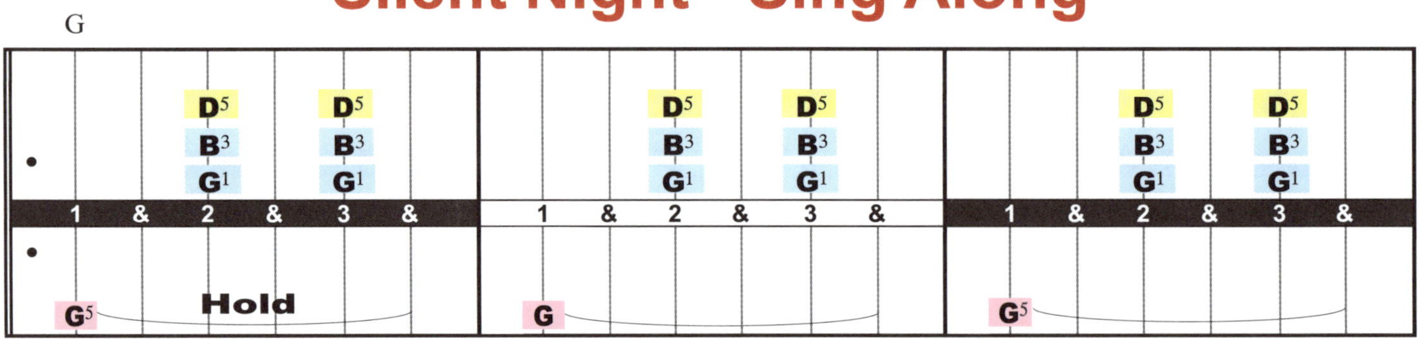

Si - lent night Ho - ly
Si - lent night Ho - ly

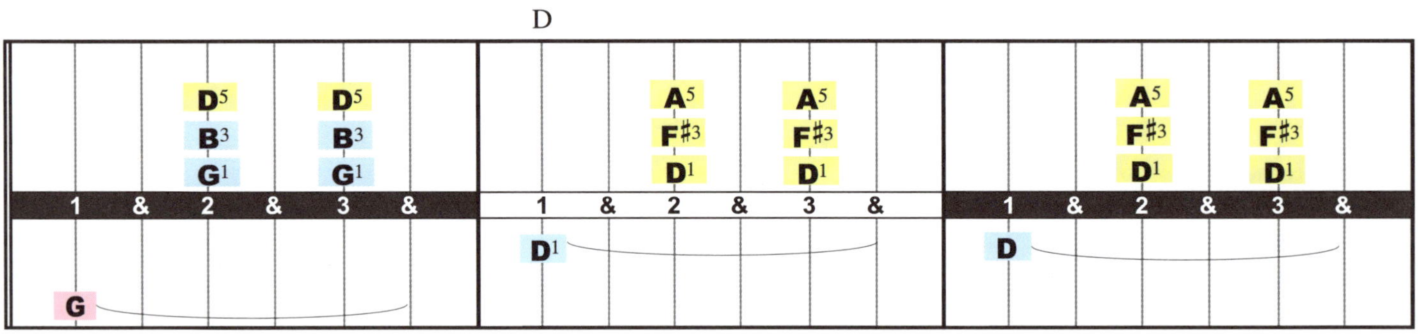

night All is calm
night She - pherds quake

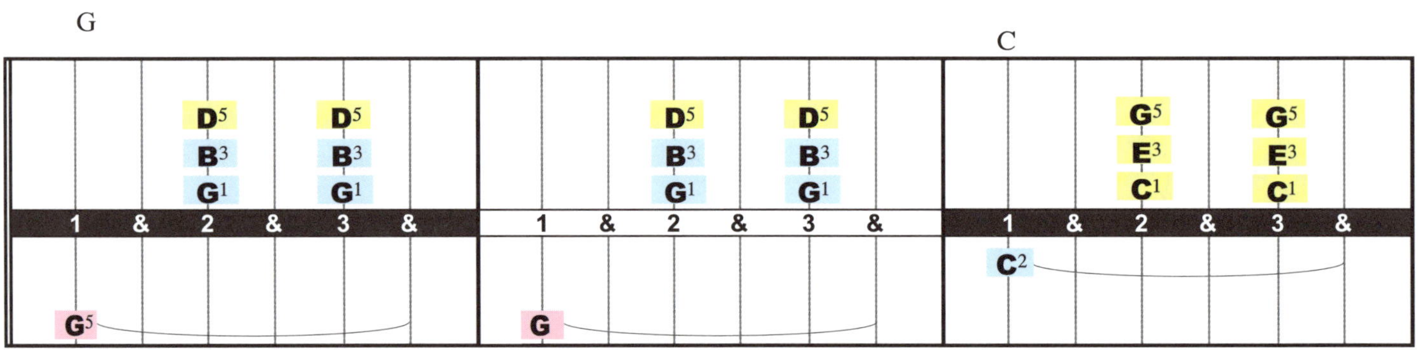

All is bright Round young
At the sight Glor - ies

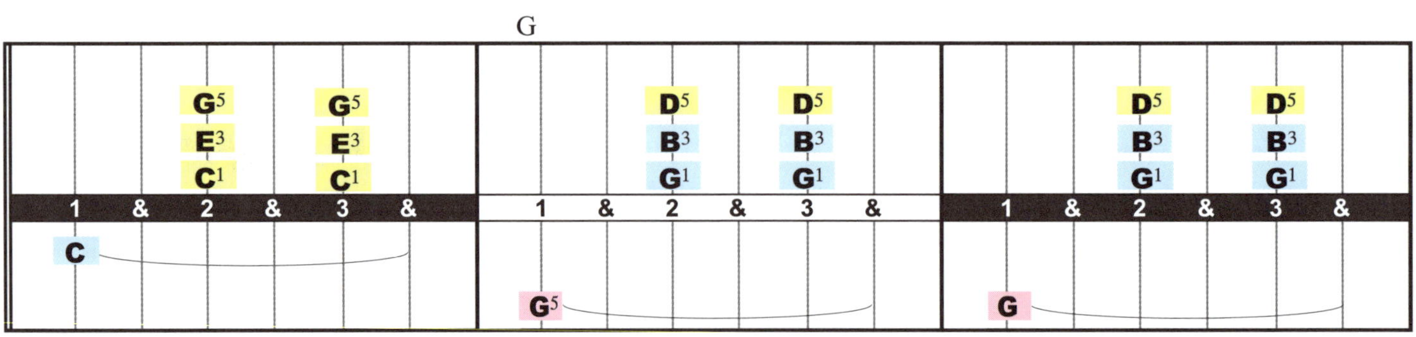

vir - gin Moth - er and child
stre - am from Hea - ven a far

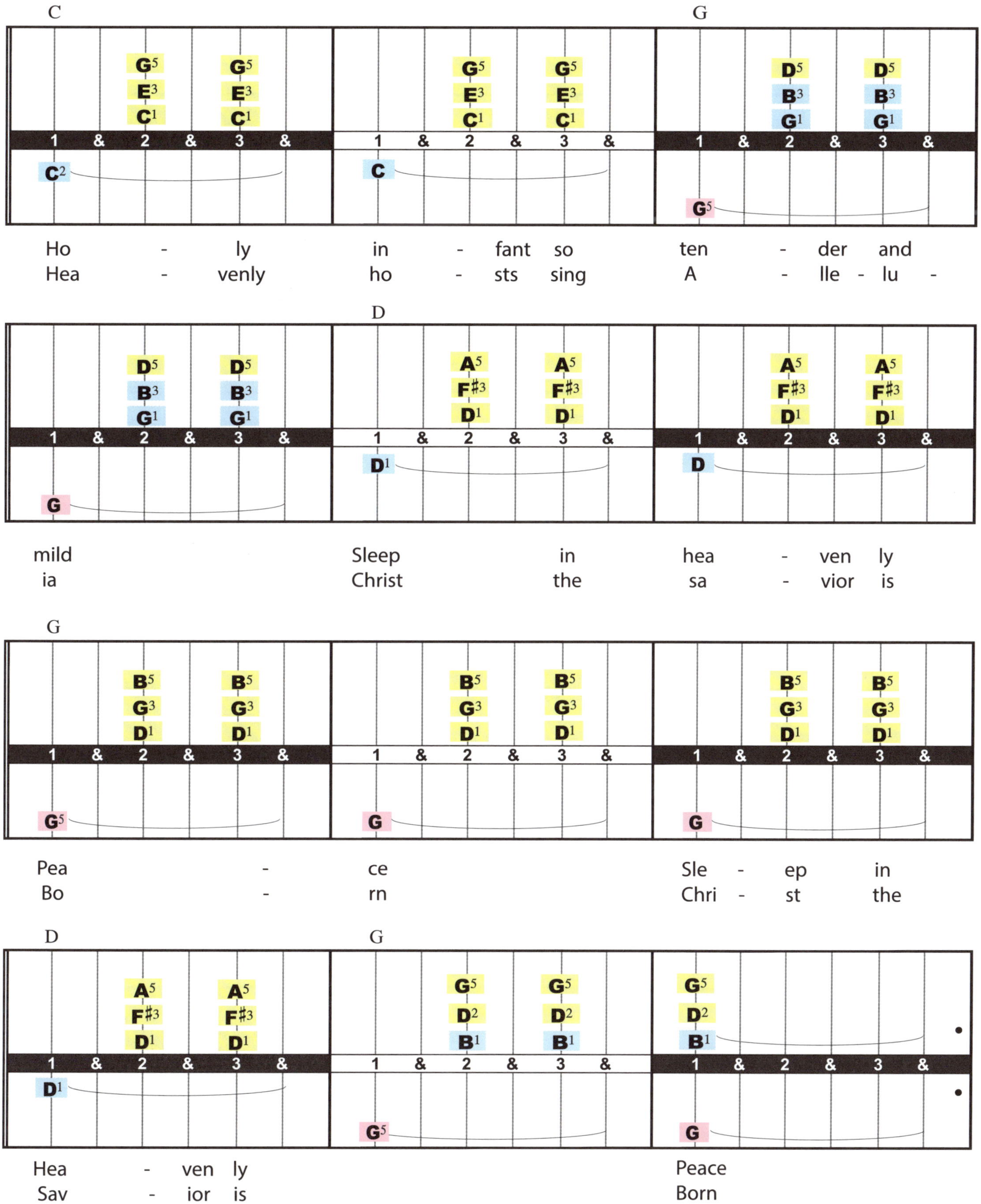
C G
Ho - ly in - fant so ten - der and
Hea - venly ho - sts sing A - lle - lu -
D
mild Sleep in hea - ven ly
ia Christ the sa - vior is
G
Pea - ce Sle - ep in
Bo - rn Chri - st the
D G
Hea - ven ly Peace
Sav - ior is Born

Jingle Bells - Sing Along

Chorus

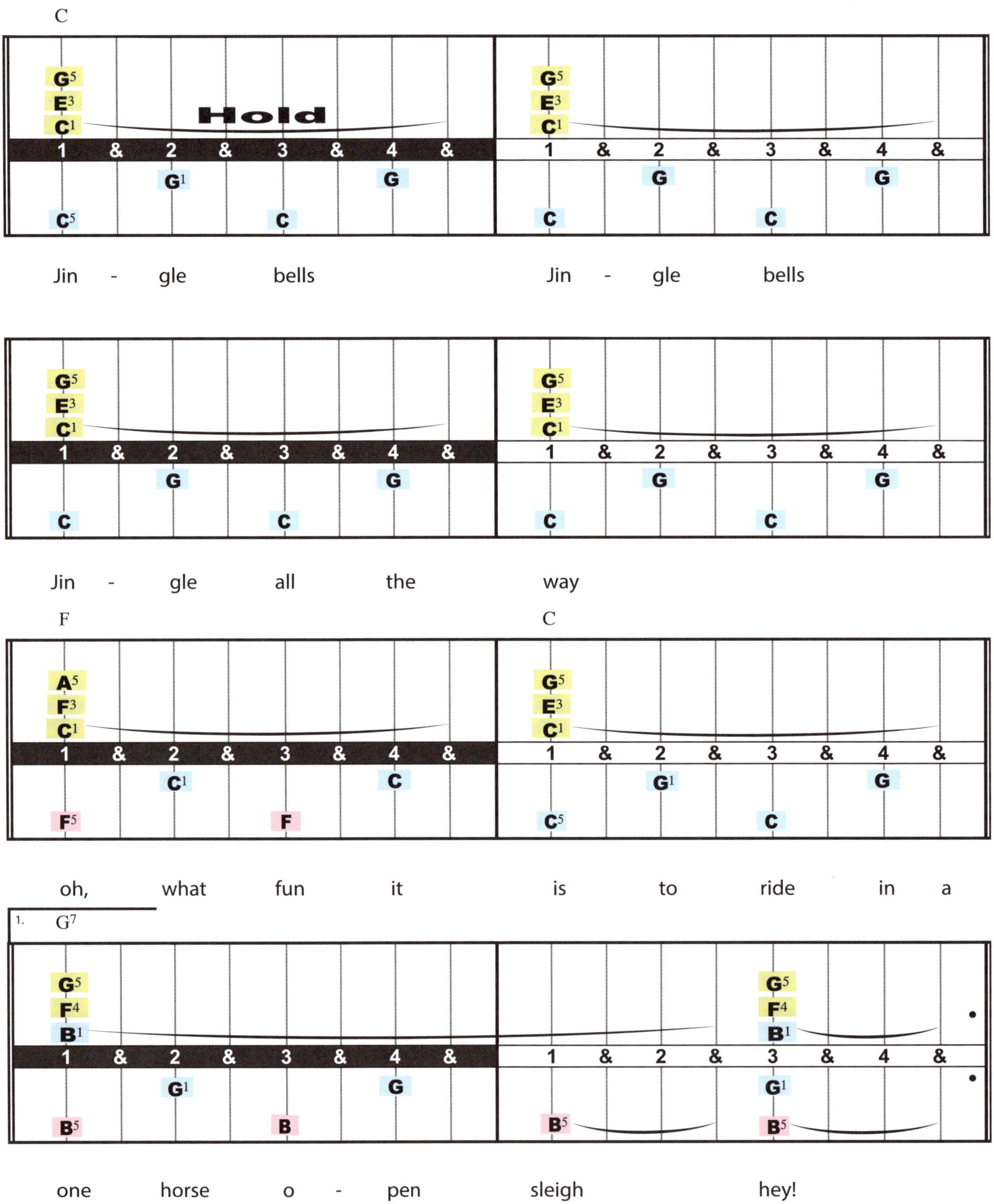

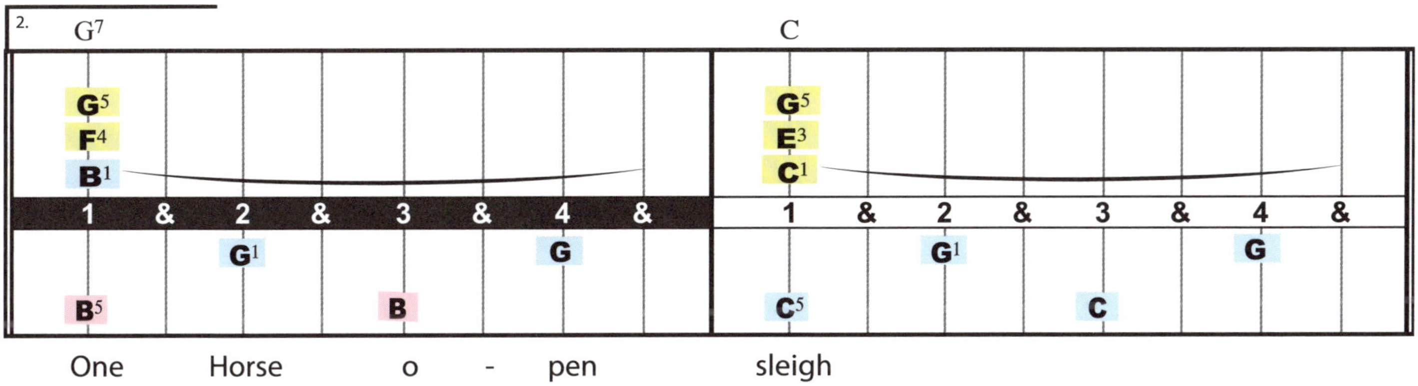
2.
G7
C
G5 F4 B1
1 & 2 & 3 & 4 &
G1 G
B5 B
G5 E3 C1
1 & 2 & 3 & 4 &
G1 G
C5 C
One Horse o - pen sleigh

Verse

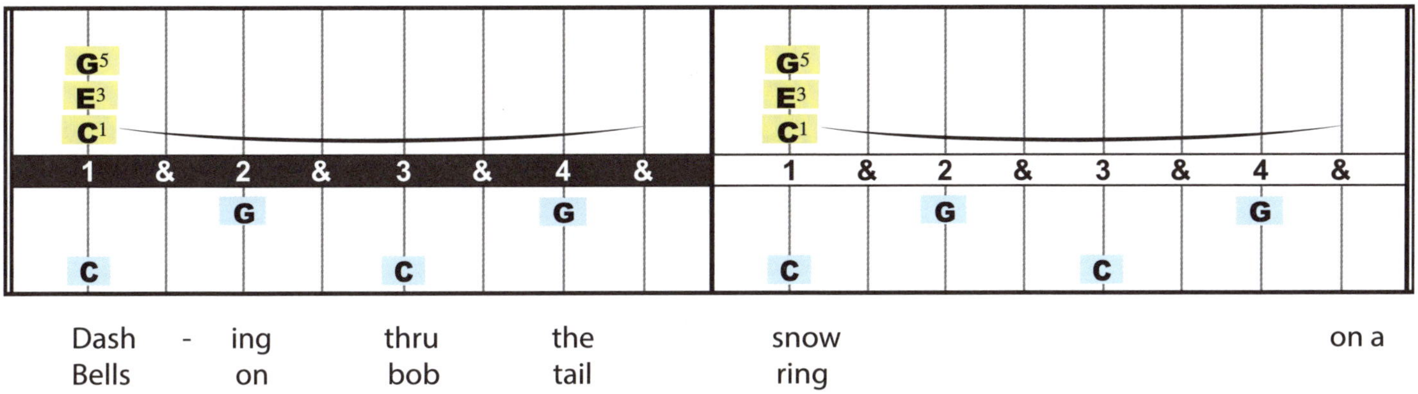
G5 E3 C1
1 & 2 & 3 & 4 &
G G
C C
G5 E3 C1
1 & 2 & 3 & 4 &
G G
C C
Dash - ing thru the snow on a
Bells on bob tail ring

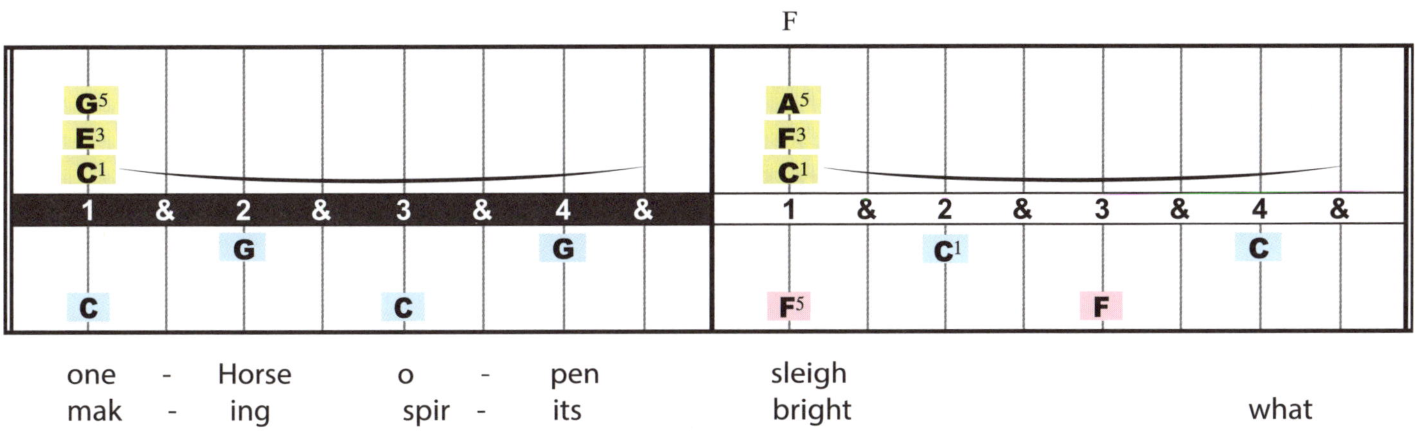
F
G5 E3 C1
1 & 2 & 3 & 4 &
G G
C C
A5 F3 C1
1 & 2 & 3 & 4 &
C1 C
F5 F
one - Horse o - pen sleigh
mak - ing spir - its bright what

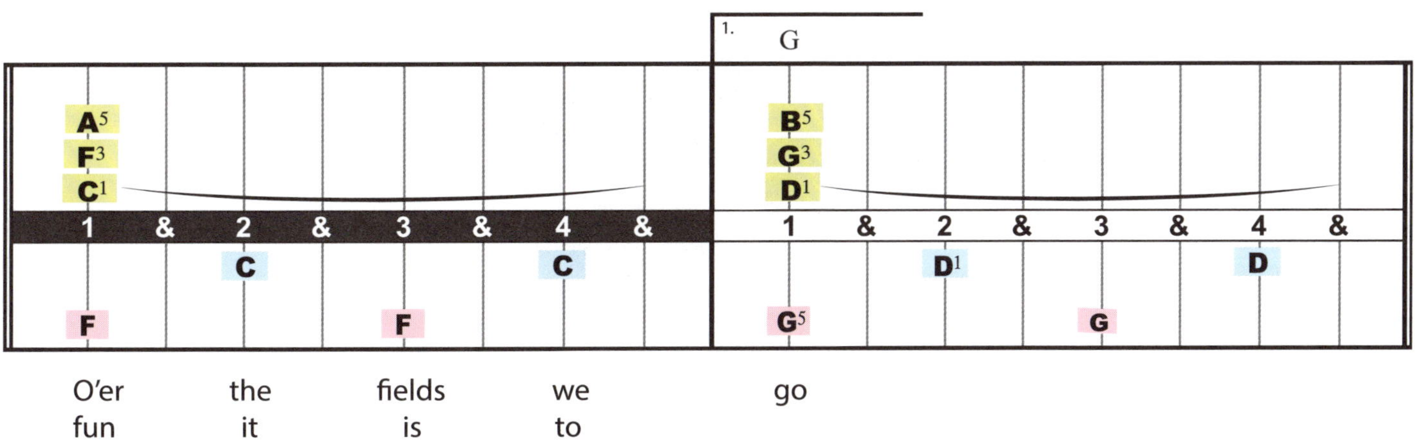
1.
G
A5 F3 C1
1 & 2 & 3 & 4 &
C C
F F
B5 G3 D1
1 & 2 & 3 & 4 &
D1 D
G5 G
O'er the fields we go
fun it is to

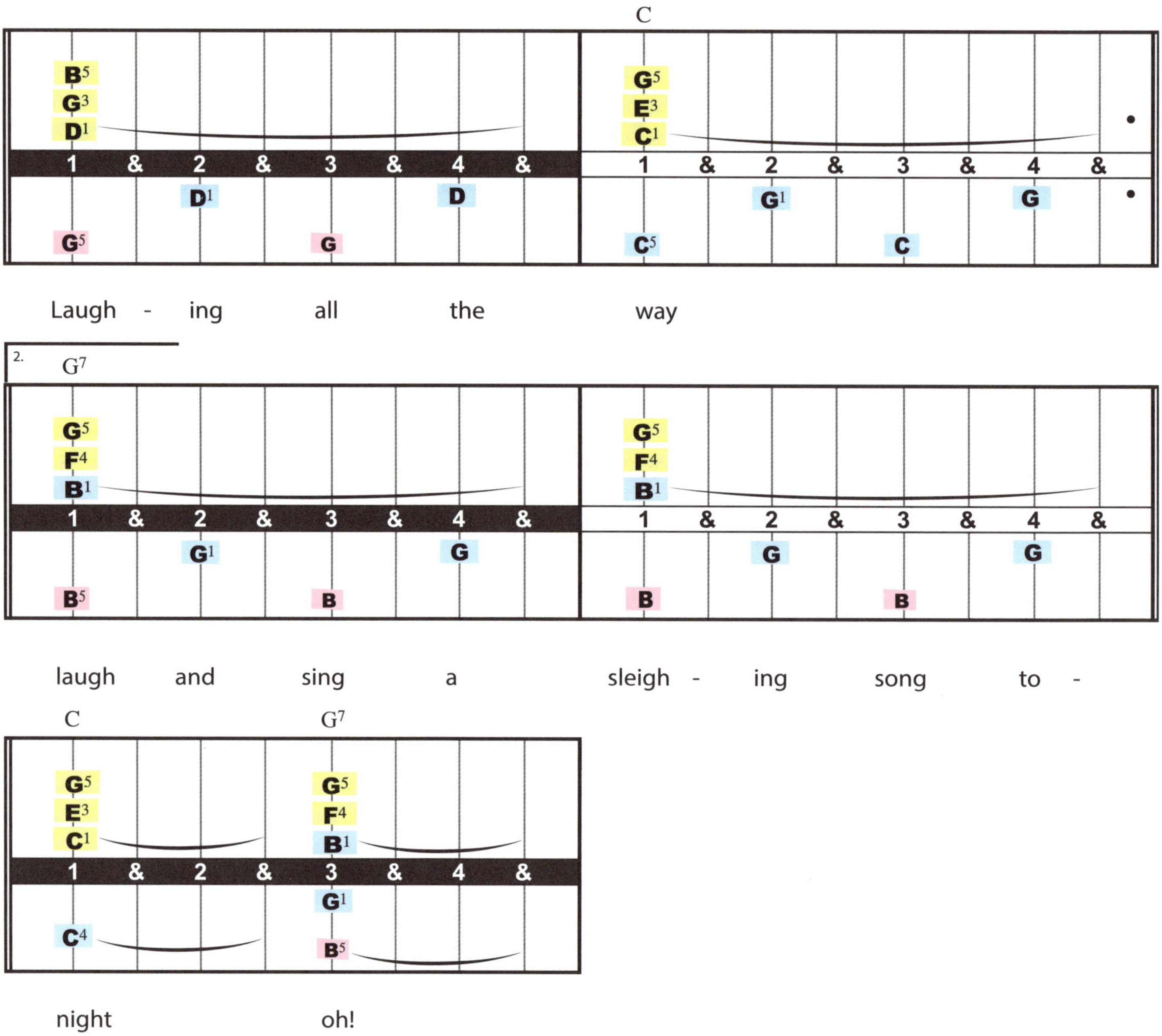
C
B5 G3 D1
1 & 2 & 3 & 4 &
D1 D
G5 G
G5 E3 C1
1 & 2 & 3 & 4 &
G1 G
C5 C
Laugh - ing all the way
2. G7
G5 F4 B1
1 & 2 & 3 & 4 &
G1 G
B5 B
G5 F4 B1
1 & 2 & 3 & 4 &
G G
B B
laugh and sing a sleigh - ing song to -
C G7
G5 E3 C1
G5 F4 B1
1 & 2 & 3 & 4 &
G1
C4
B5
night oh!

Santa Claus is Coming to Town - Sing Along

Verse

G C II G C II

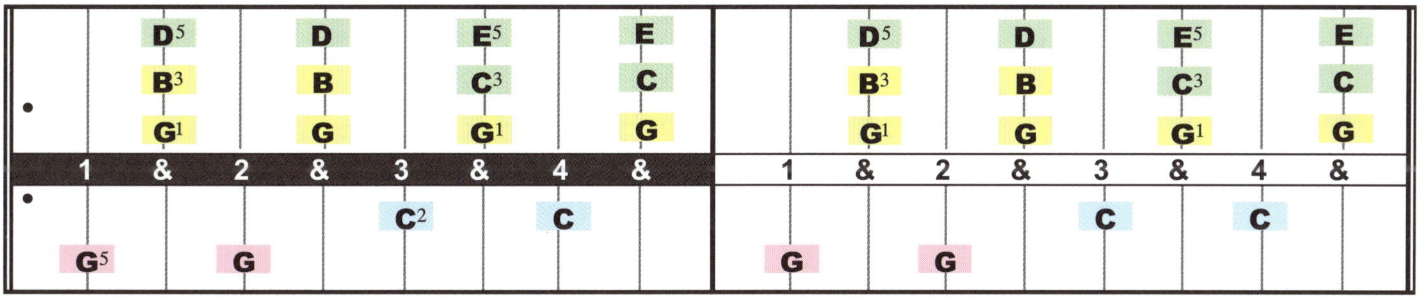

You Better watch out You Better not cry you better not pout I'm telling you why
He's making a list he's checking it twice he's gonna find out who's naughty or nice

G Em Am II D G

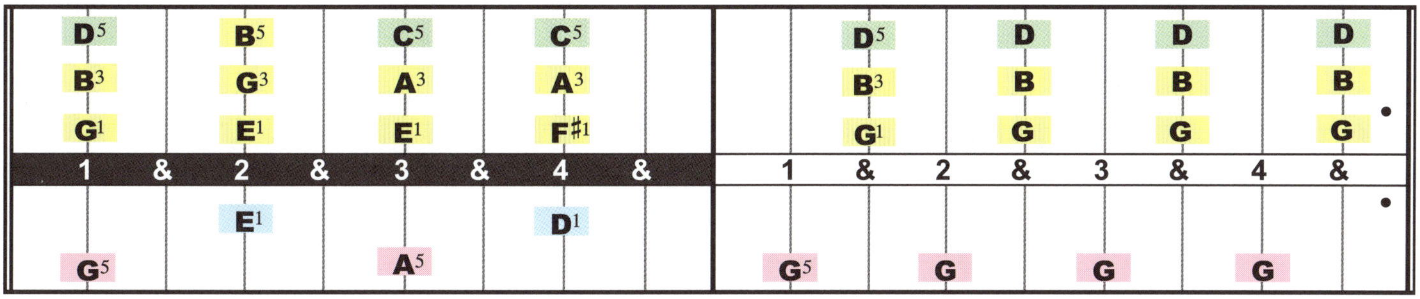

San - ta clause is com - ing to town
San - ta clause is com - ing to town he

Bridge

G^7 C II G^7 C II

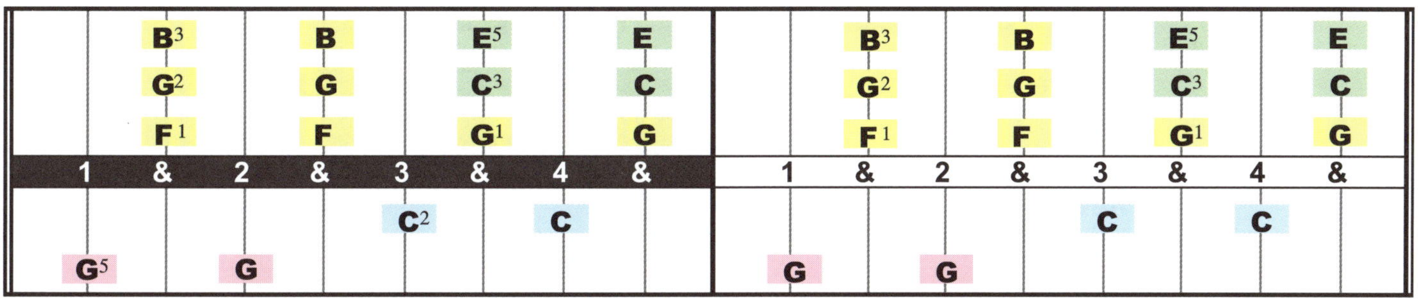

sees you when you're sleep - ing he knows when you're a - wake he
The Kids in girl and Boy - land will have a ju - bi - lee They're

A D II

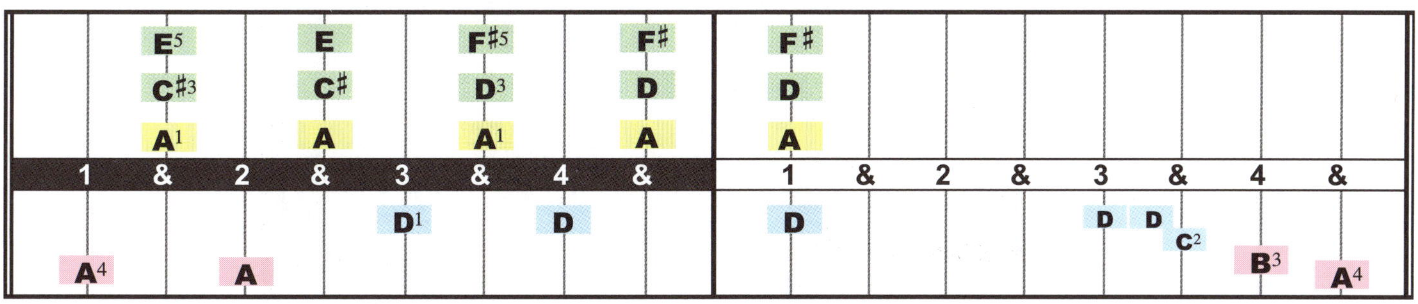

knows when you've been bad or good so be good for good - ness sake So
gon - na build a toy - land all a - round the christ - mas tree So

Chorus

G CII G CII

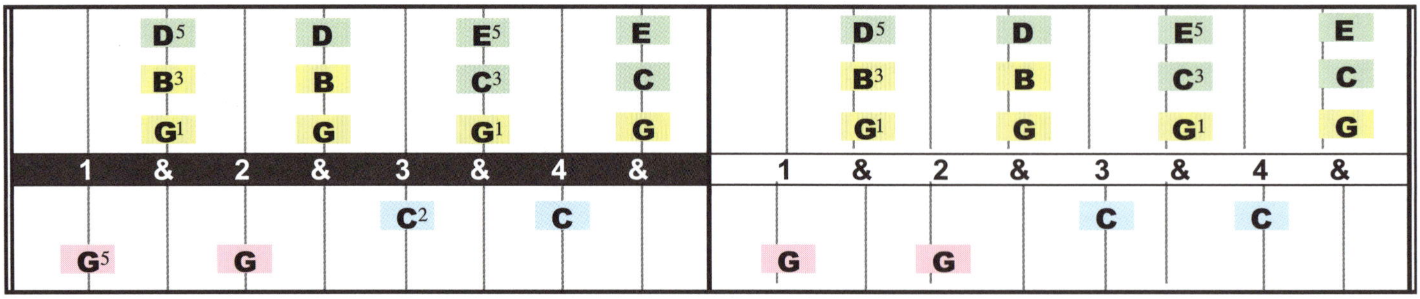

You Better watch out You Better not cry you better not pout I'm telling you why

G Em Am II D^7 G

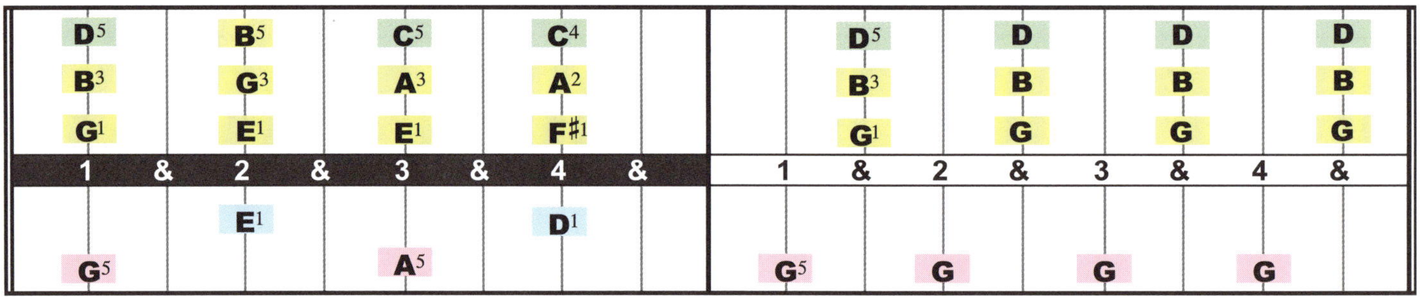

San - ta clause is com - ing to town

Structure

Verse - Verse - Bridge - Chorus - Verse

Verse - Bridge - Chorus - Bridge - Chorus 2x

Verse 2

Little tin horns, little tin drums
Rudy-toot-toot and rummy tum tums
Santa Claus is comin' to town

Verse 3

And curly head dolls that cuddle and coo
Elephants, boats and kiddy cars too
Santa Claus is comin' to town

We Wish You a Merry Christmas - Sing Along

Verse

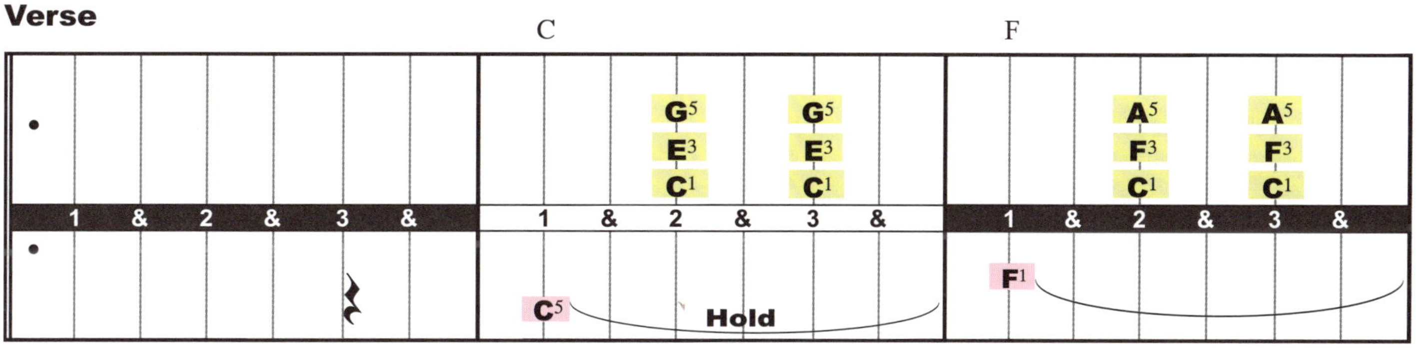

1. We wish you a Mer - ry Christ - mas we
2. Now bring us some fig - gy pud - ding now

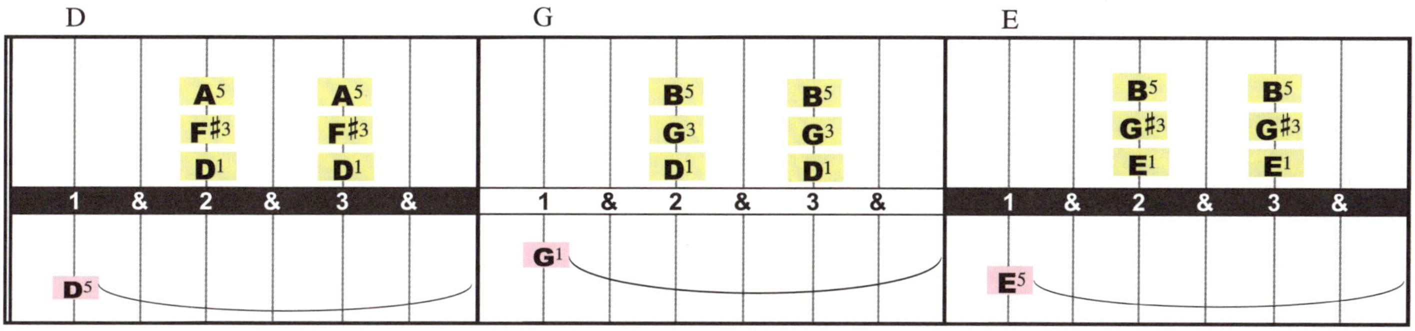

wish you a Mer - ry Christ - mas we wish you a mer - ry
bring us some fig - gy pud - ding now bring us some fig - gy

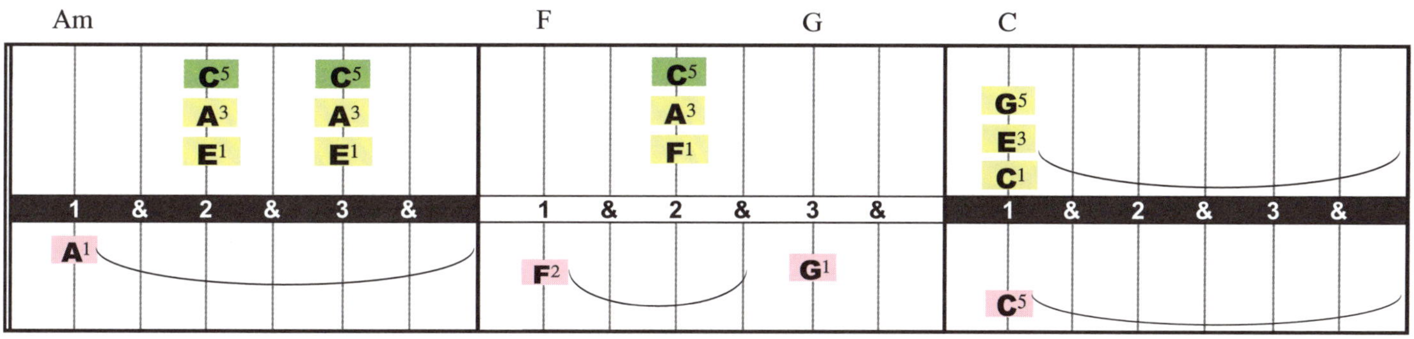

Christ - mas and a hap - py new year good
pud - ding now bring some out now good

Refrain

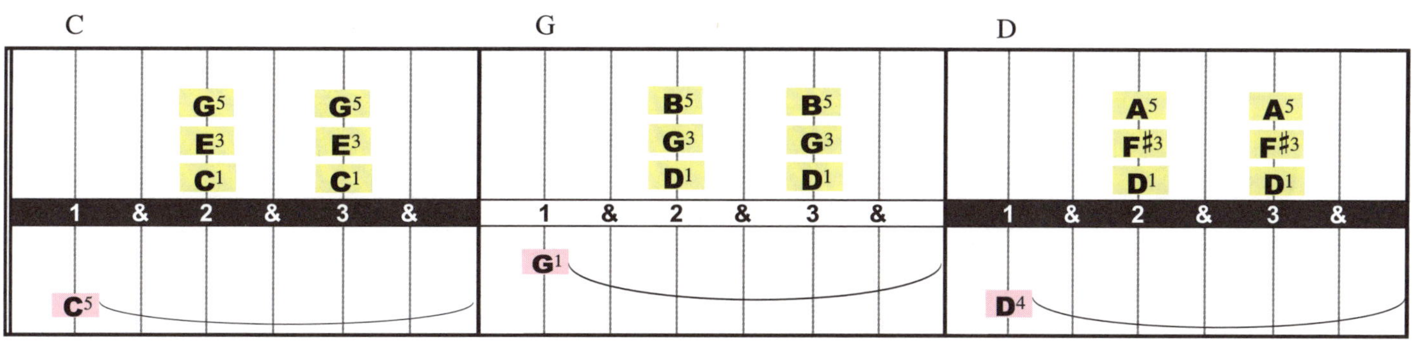

ti - dings we bring for you and your

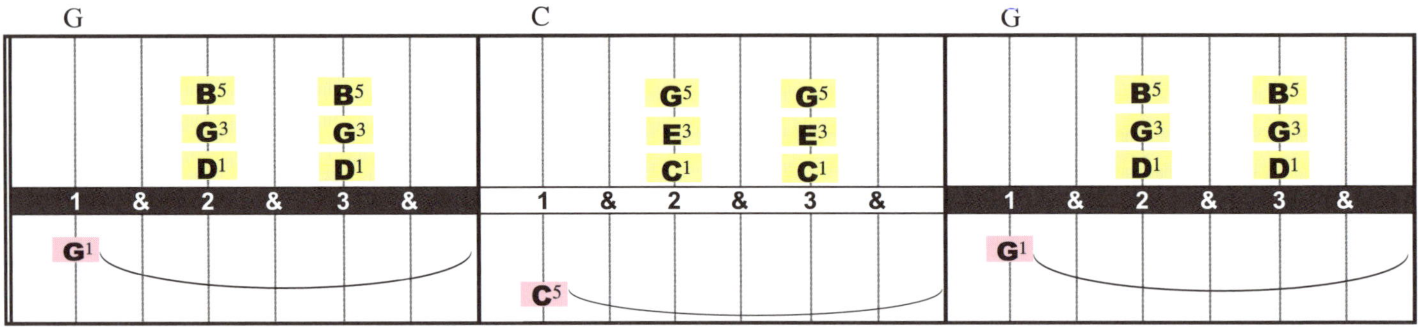

kin we wish you a Mer - ry Christ - mas and a

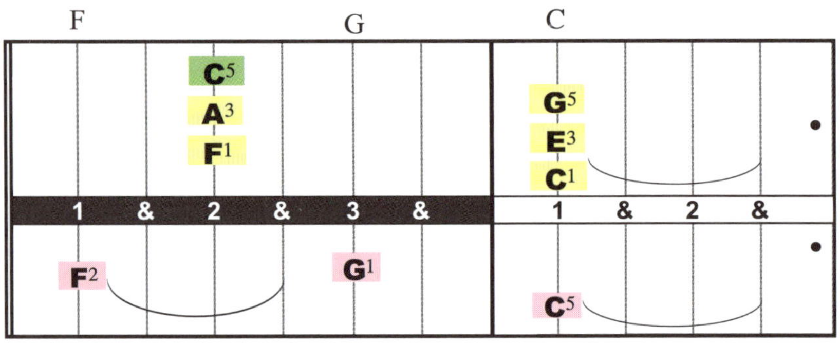

ha - py new year

Verse 3
We wont go until we get some
We wont go until we get some
We wont go until we get some
So bring it right here

Verse 4
We all like our figgy pudding
We all like our figgy pudding
We all like our figgy pudding
With all its good cheers

Rudolph the Red-Nosed Reindeer
Sing Along

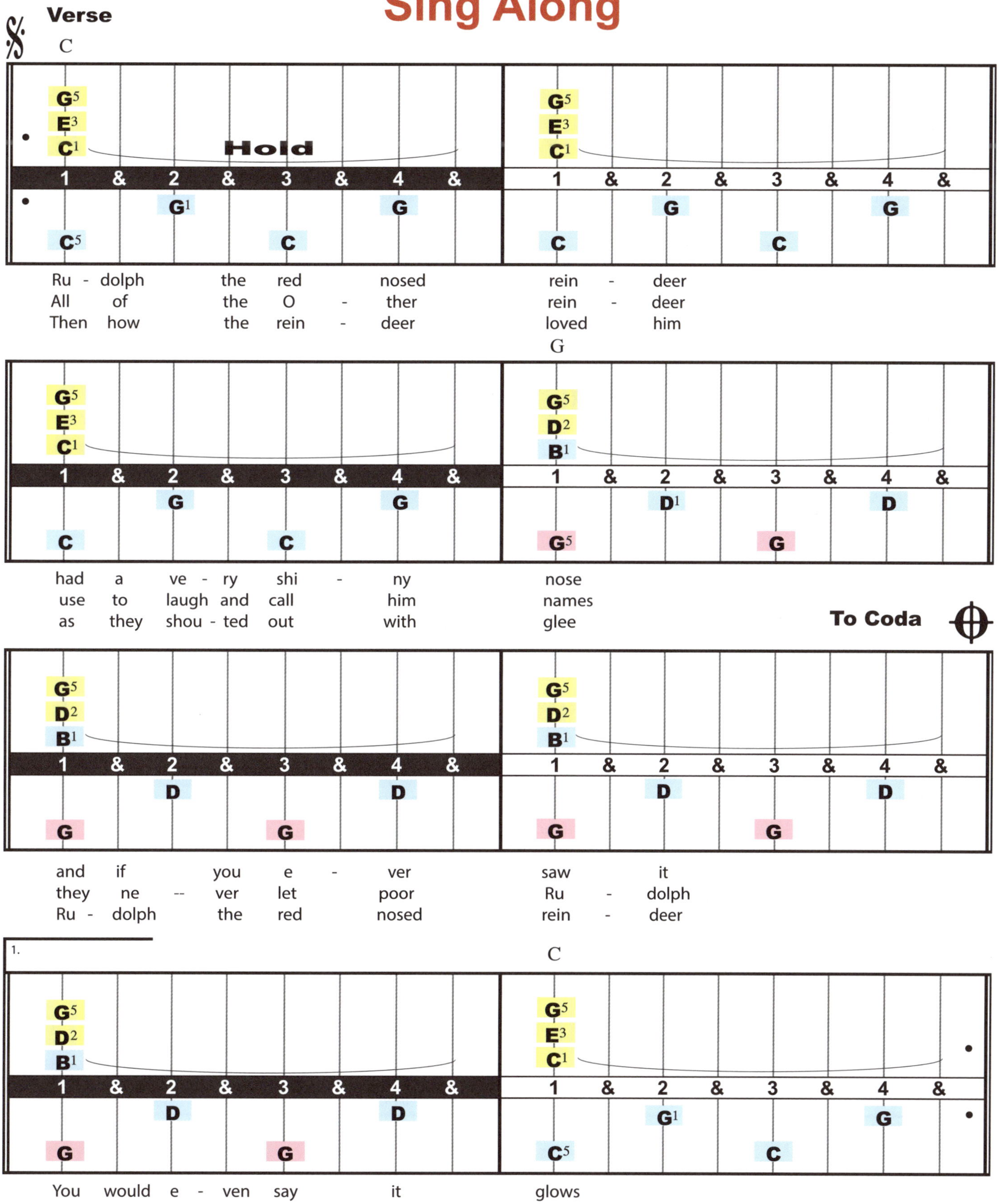

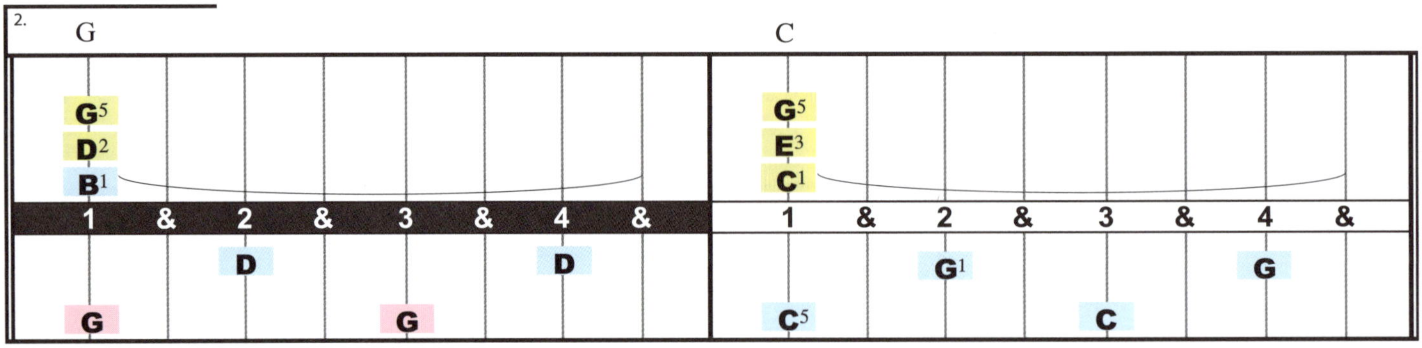

join in an - y rein - deer games

Bridge

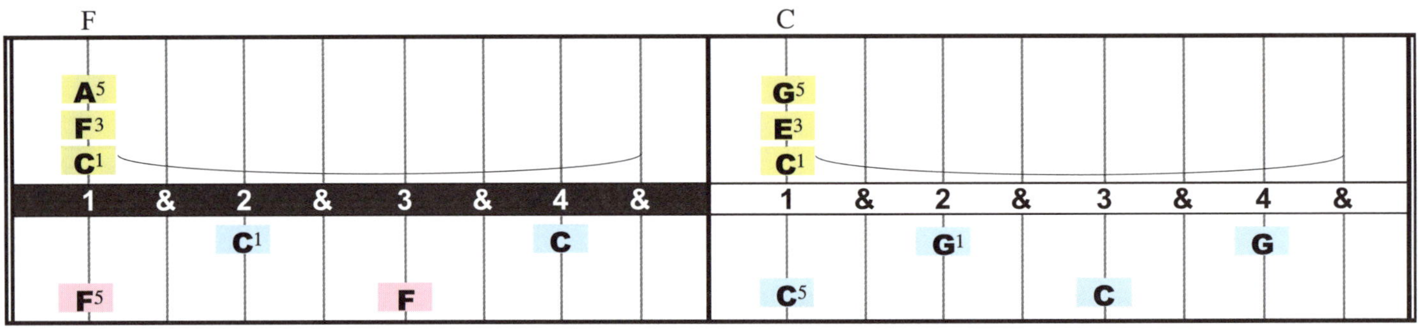

Then one fog - gy Christ - mas eve

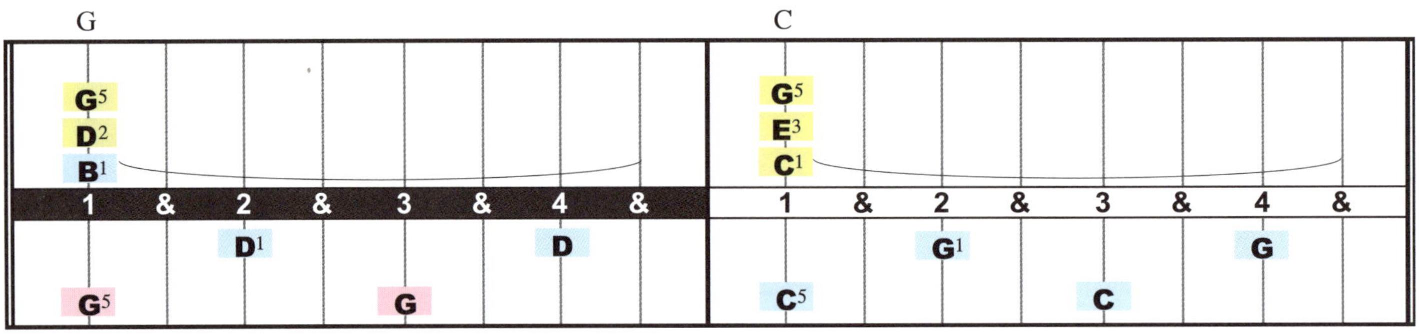

San - ta came to say

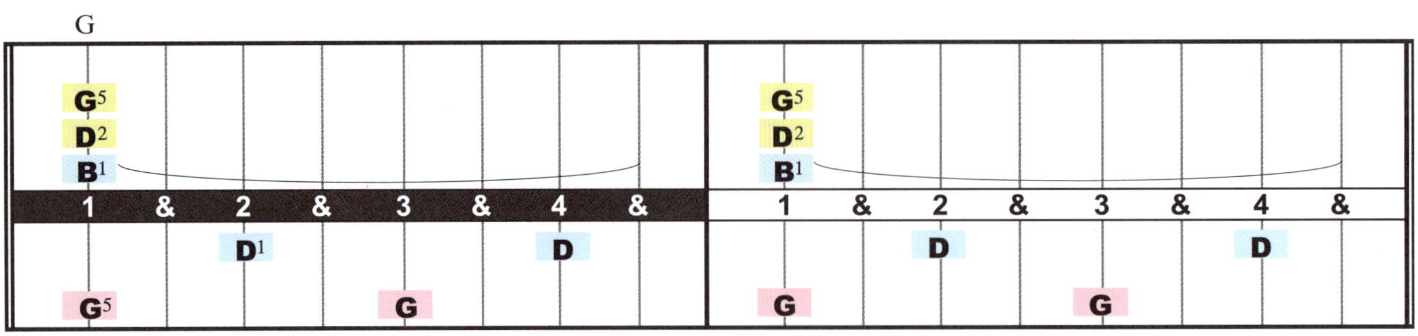

"Ru - dolph with your nose so bright

D.S. Al Coda

D7								G							
A5 D2 C1								G5 D2 B1							
1	&	2	&	3	&	4	&	1	&	2	&	3	&	4	&
A1 D5								D1 G5							
wont			you	guide		my		sleigh		to	- night ?“				

Coda

G								C							
G5 D2 B1								G5 E3 C1							
1	&	2	&	3	&	4	&	1	&	2	&	3	&	4	&
		D1				D		G1							
G5				G				C5							
you'll	go	down	in	his	-	to	-	ry							

Structure

Verse - Bridge - Verse - Coda

We Three Kings - Sing Along

Verse

Am G

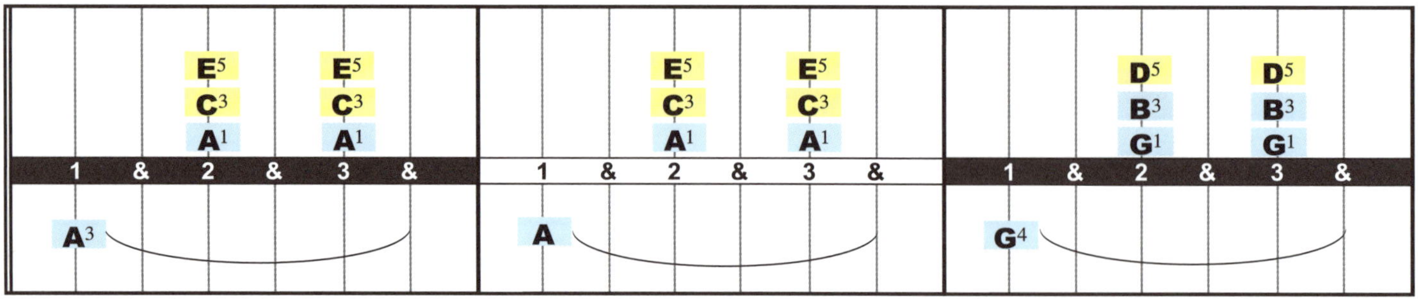

We Three Kings of or - ie - nt

Am

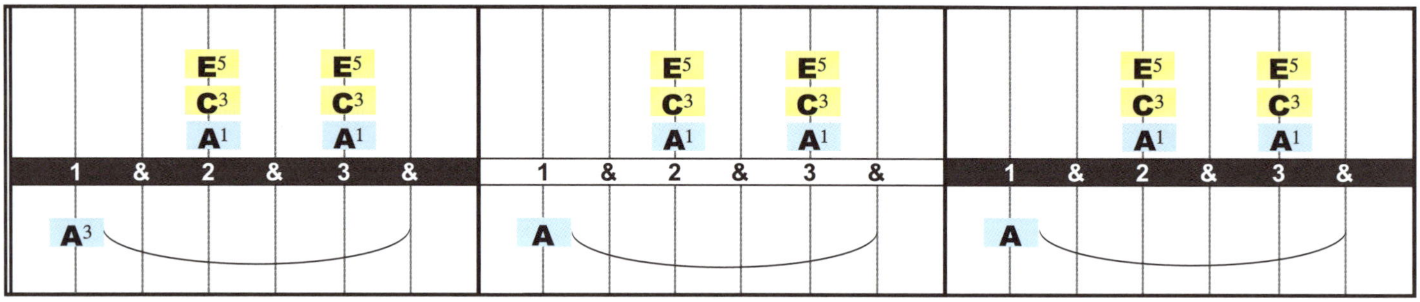

are Bear - ing gifts we

G Am

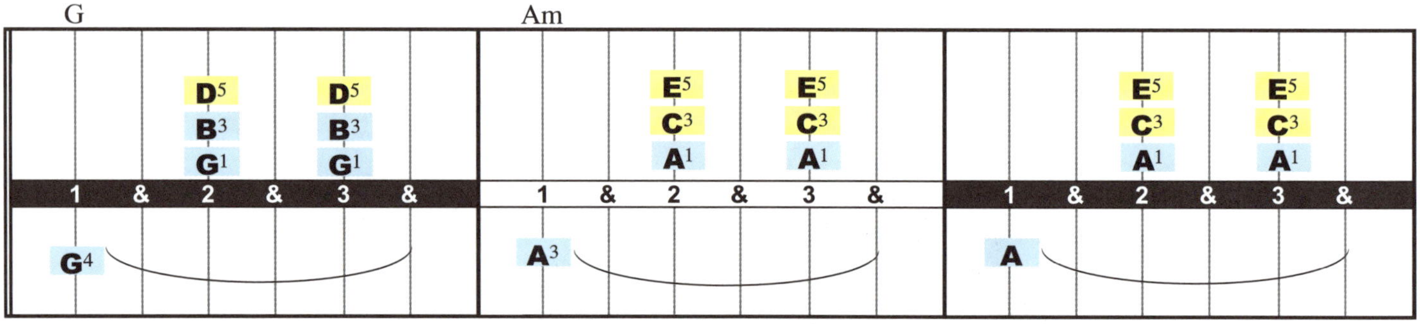

tra - verse a - far field and

G C

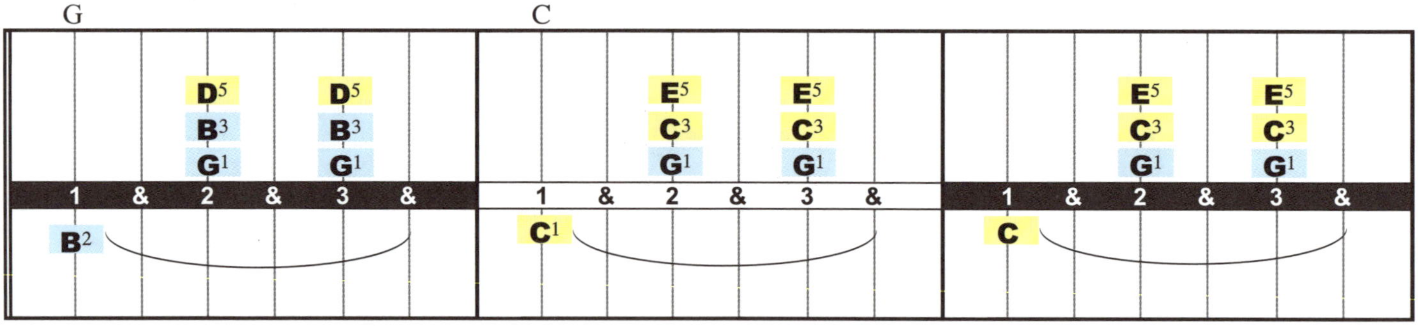

foun - tain moor and mo - un - tain

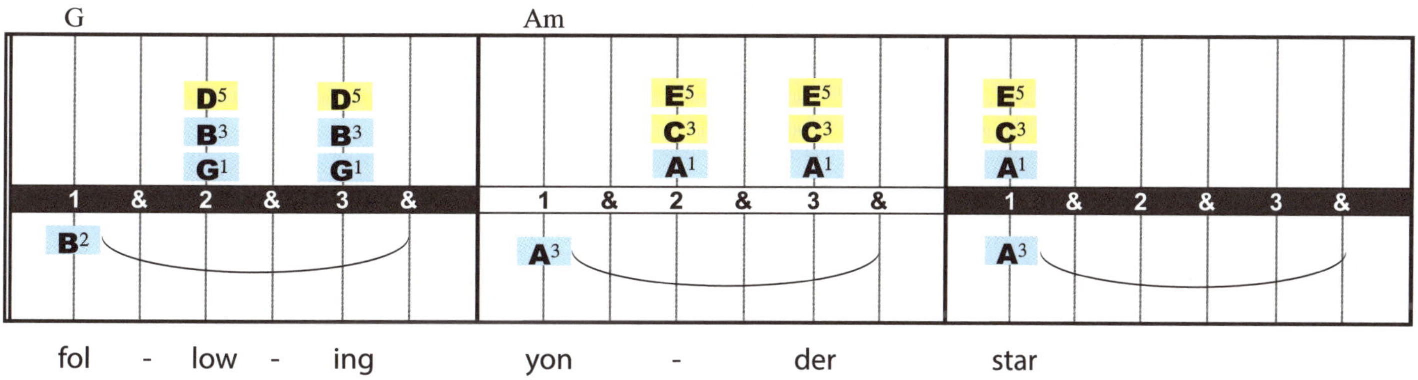

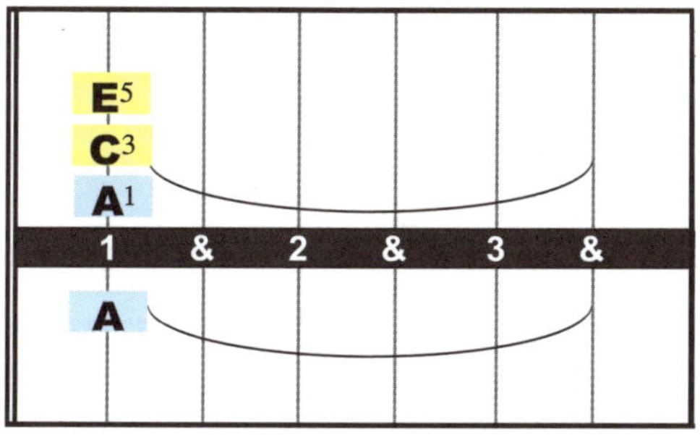

Verse 2
Born a King on Bethlehem's plain
Gold I bring to crown Him again
King for ever, ceasing never
Over us all to reign

Verse 3
Frankincense to offer have I
Incense owns a Deity nigh
Prayer and praising, all men raising worship
Him, God most high

Verse 4
Myrrh is mine Its bitter perfume
Breathes a life of gathering gloom
Sorrowing, sighing, bleeding, dying
Sealed in the stone cold tomb

Verse 5
Glorious now behold Him arise
King and God and Sacrifice!
Al-le-lu-ia, al-le-lu-ia
Heaven to earth replies

I Saw Three Ships - Sing Along

Verse

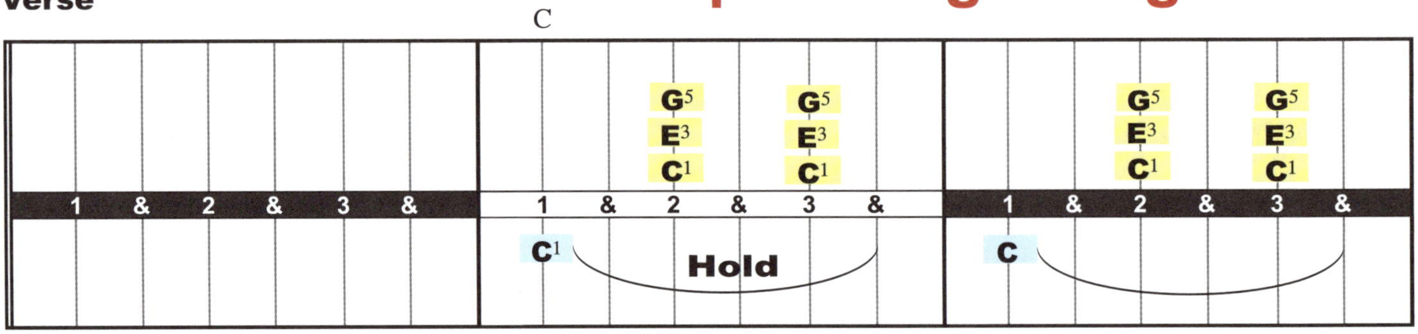

I saw three ships come

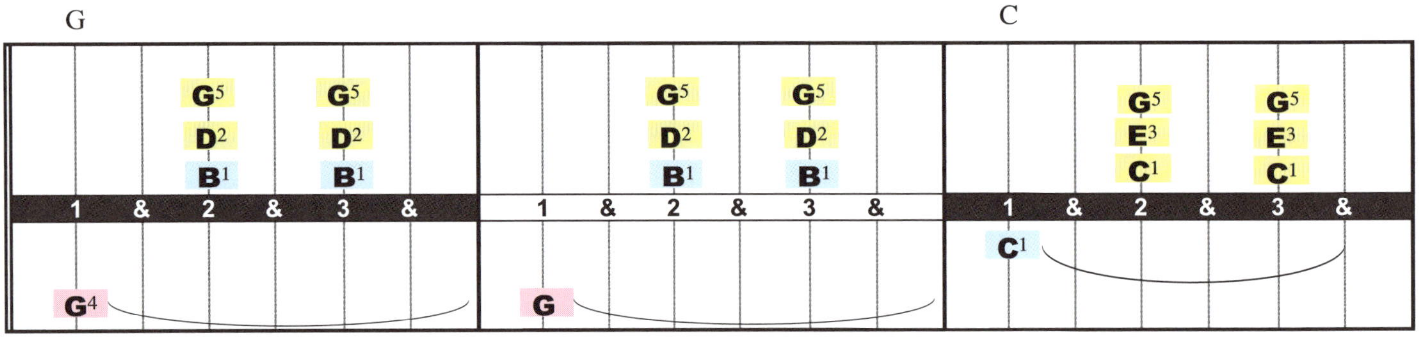

sail - ing in, on Christ - mas

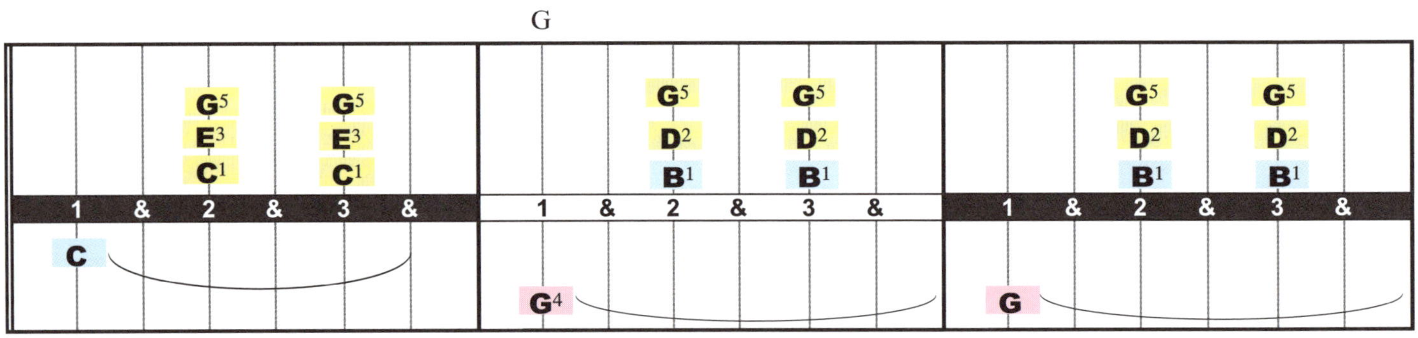

Day on Christ - mas Day I

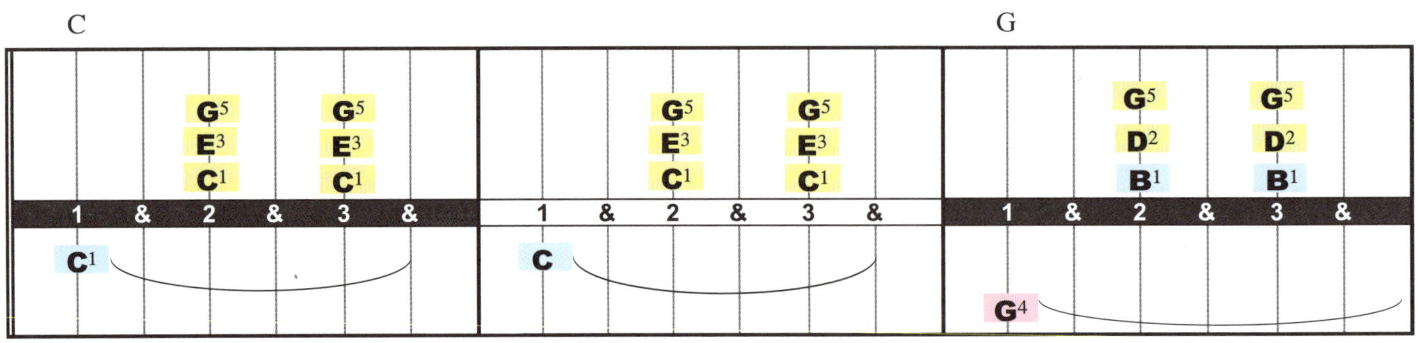

saw three ships come sail - ing

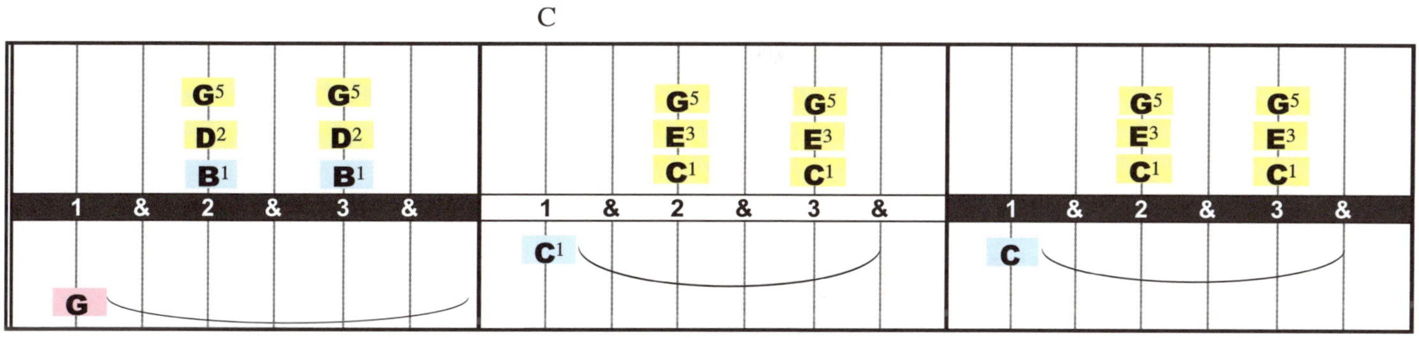

in, on Christ - mas Day in the

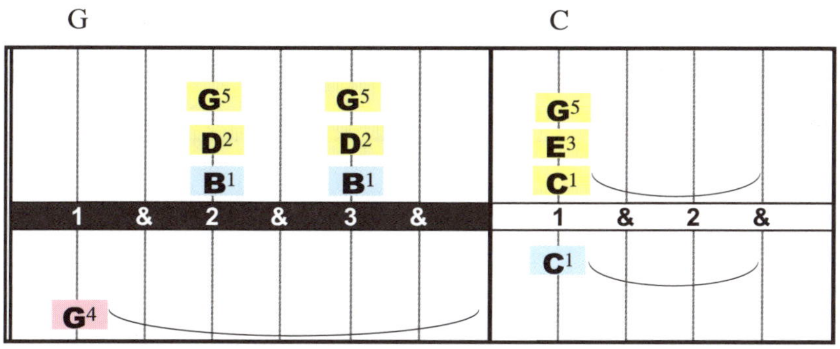

morn - ing

Verse 2

And what was in those ships all three
On Christmas Day, on Christmas Day?
And what was in those ships all three
On Christmas Day in the morning?

Verse 3

Frankincense to offer have I
Incense owns a Deity nigh
Prayer and praising, all men raising worship
Him, God most high

Verse 4

And all the bells on Earth shall ring
On Christmas Day, on Christmas Day
And all the bells on Earth shall ring
On Christmas Day in the morning

Verse 5

And all the angels in Heaven shall sing
On Christmas Day, on Christmas Day
And all the angels in Heaven shall sing
On Christmas Day in the morning

Verse 6

Then let us all rejoice again
On Christmas Day, on Christmas Day
Then let us all rejoice again
On Christmas Day in the morning

Frosty The Snow Man - Sing Along

Verse

C

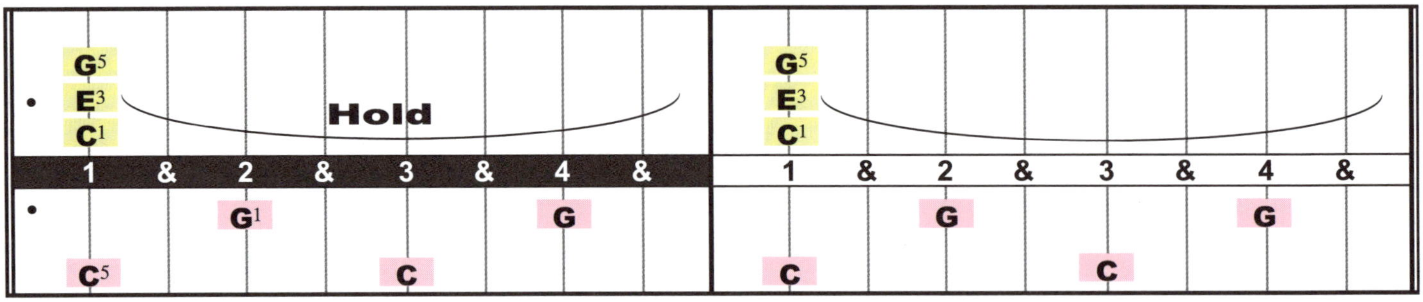

1. Fros - ty the snow man was a
2. Fros - ty the snow man is a

F C

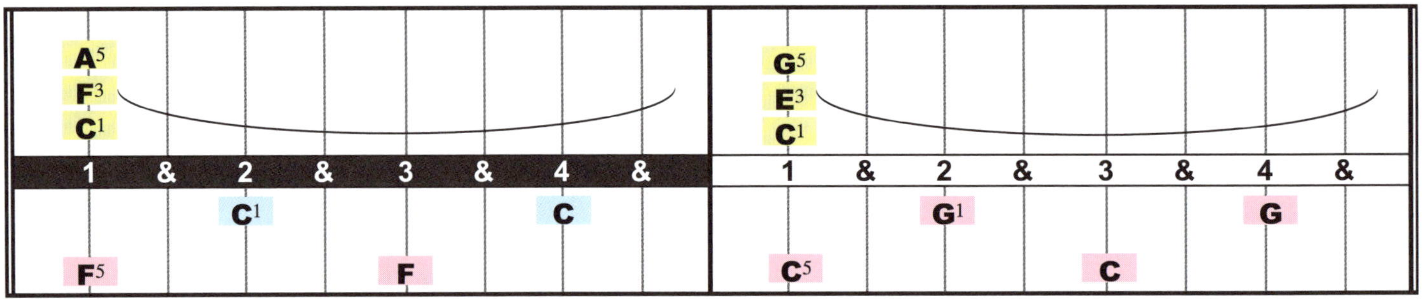

jol - ly hap - py soul with a
fai - ry tail they say he was

F C

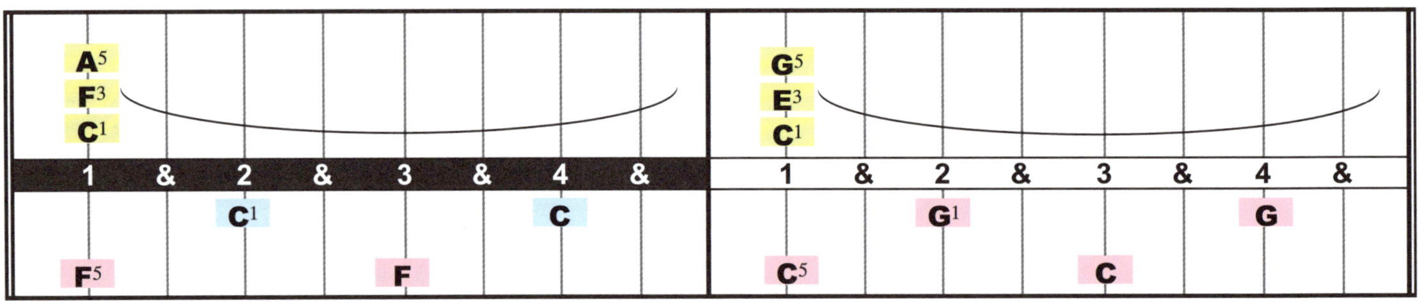

corn cob pipe and a but - ton nose and two
made of snow but the Chil - dren know how he

1. 4. G C

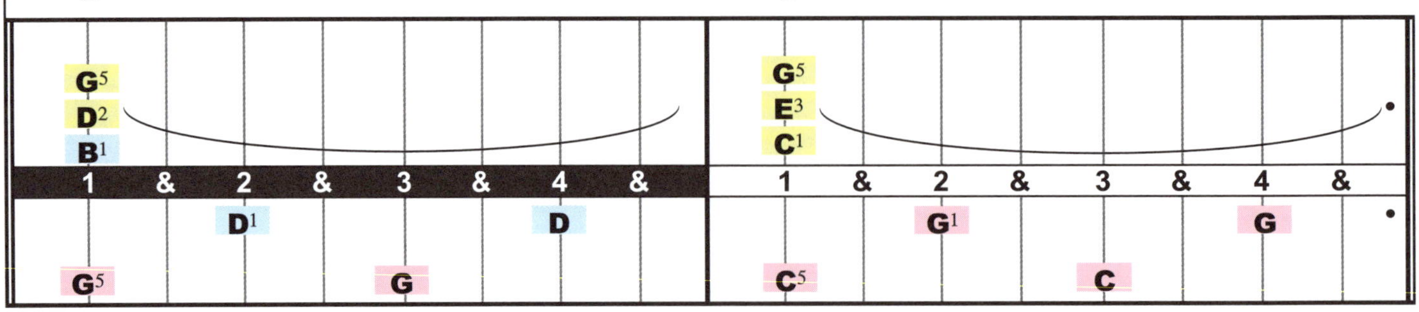

eyes made out of coal

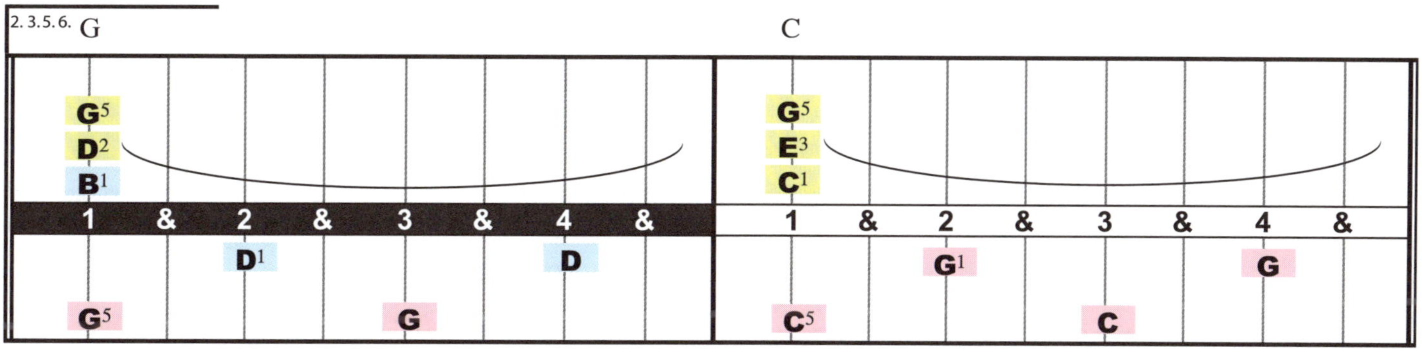

came to life one day There
He

Bridge

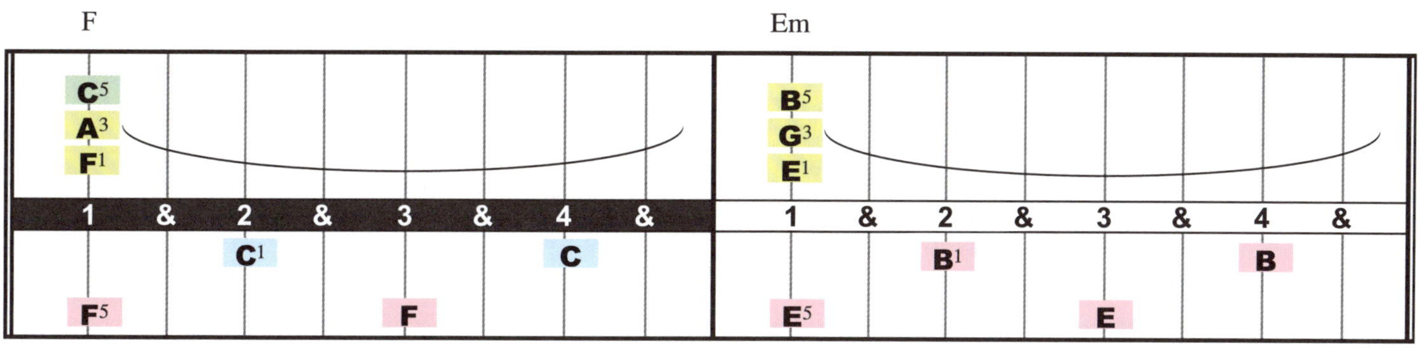

1. Must have been some ma - gic in that
2. led them down the streets of town right

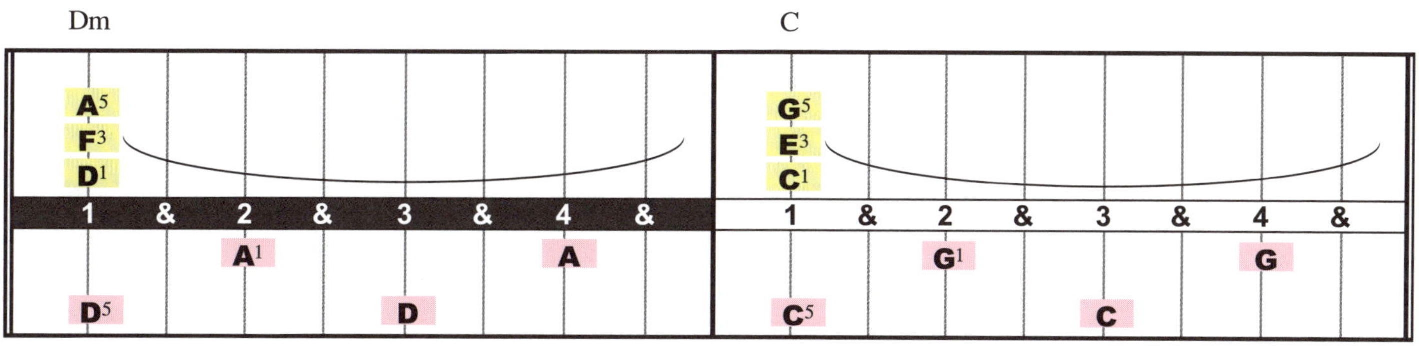

old top hat they found for
to the traf - fic cop he

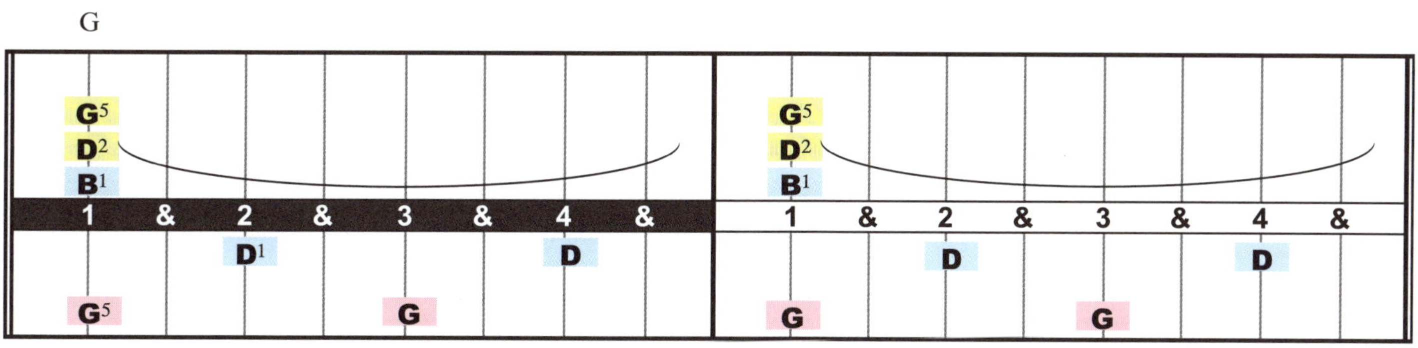

when they placed it on his head he be -
on - ly paused a mo - ment when he

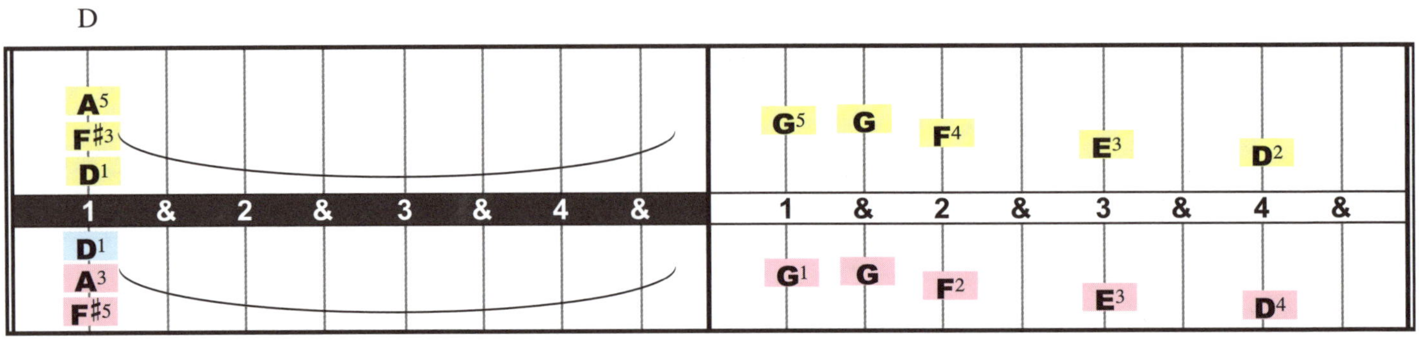

- gan to dance a - round oh
heard him holl - ar "stop!" oh

Chorus

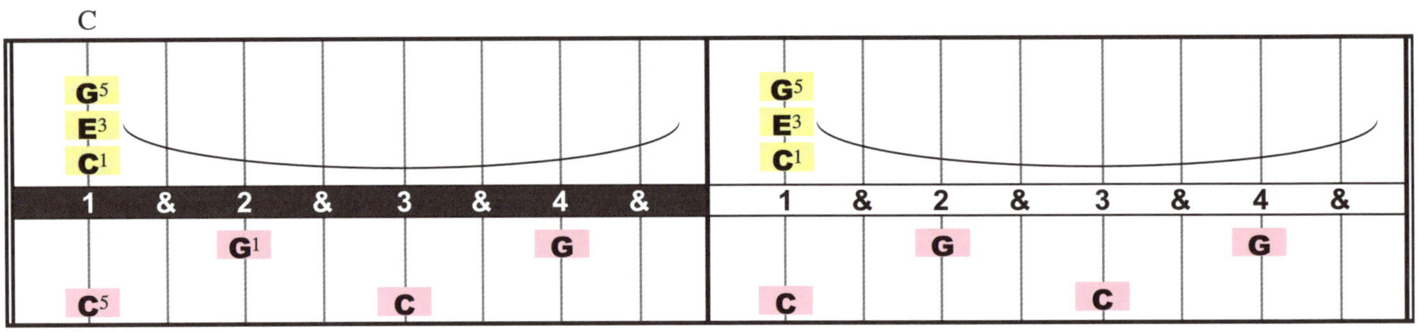

Thum - pe - ty Thump Thump Thum - pe - ty Thump Thump

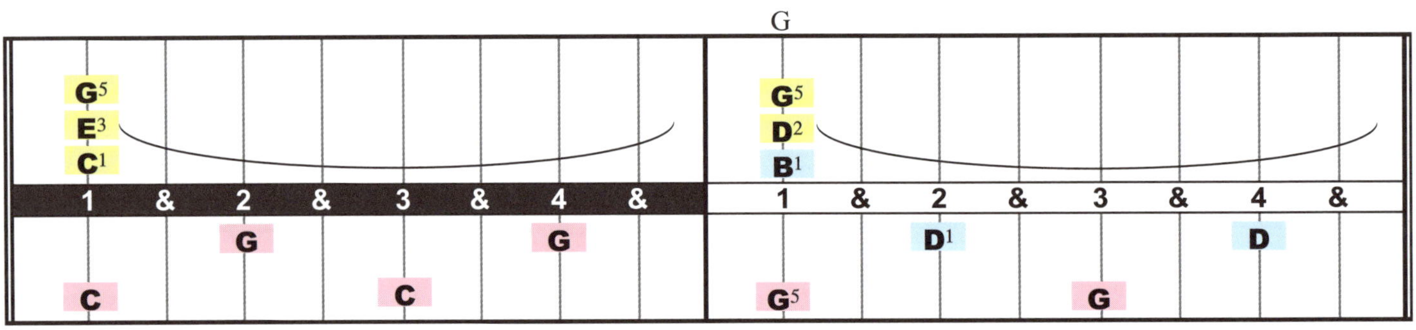

Look at Fros - ty go

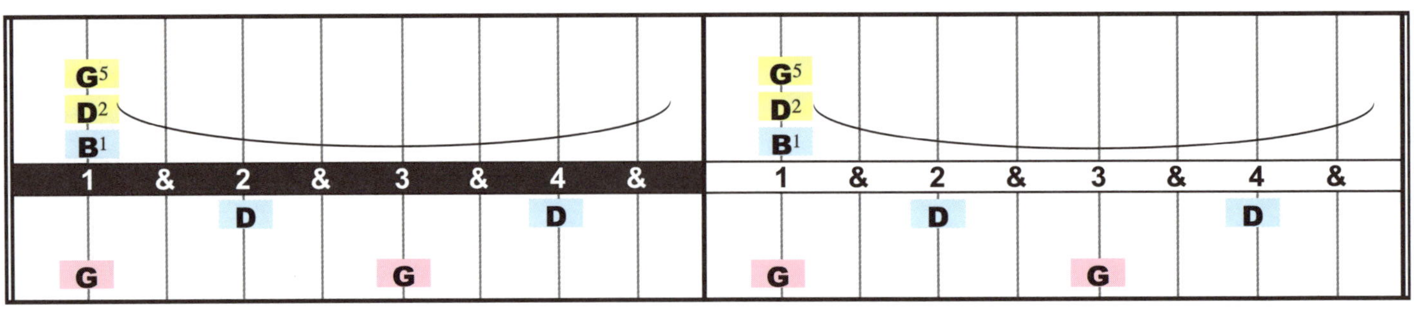

Thum - pe - ty Thump Thump Thum - pe - ty Thump Thump

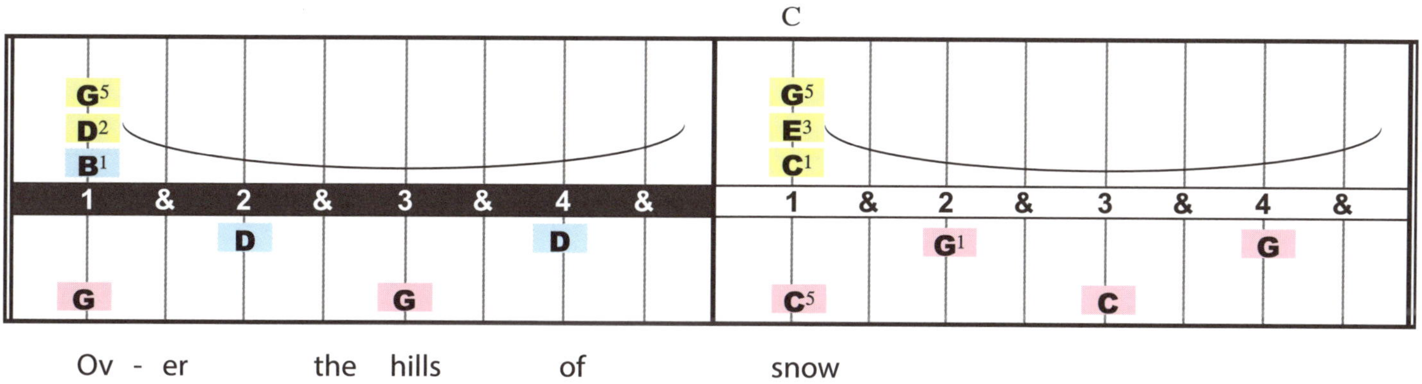

Structure

Verse - Verse - Bridge - Verse - Chorus - Verse - Verse - Bridge - Verse

Verse 3
Frosty the snowman, was alive
As he could be and the
Children say he could laugh
And play just the same as you and me

Verse 4
Oh Frosty the snowman knew
The sun was hot that day. So
He said, “Let’s run and we’ll
Have some fun now before I melt away!”

Verse 5
Down to the village with a
Broomstick in his hand. Running
Here and there all around the
Square saying “Catch me if you can!”

Verse 6
Oh, Frosty the snowman had to
Hurry on his way. But he waved
Goodbye, saying “Don’t you cry, I’ll
Be back again someday.”

Deck the Halls - Sing Along

Verse A

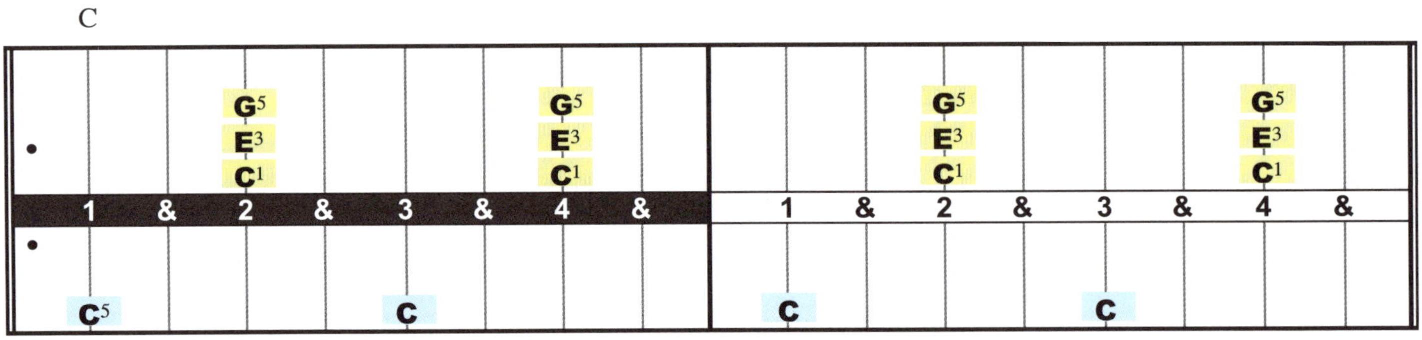

Deck the halls with boughs of hol - ly
Tis the sea - son to be jol - ly

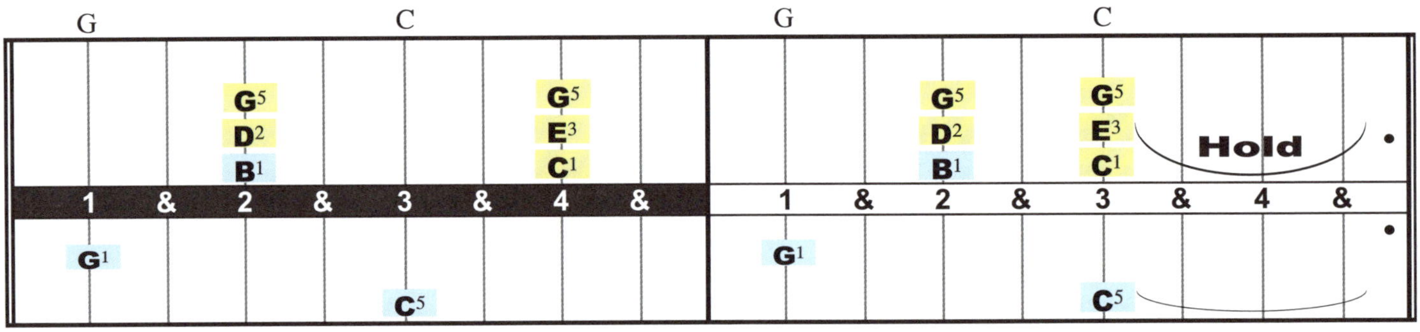

Fa la la la la la la la la
Fa la la la la la la la la

Bridge

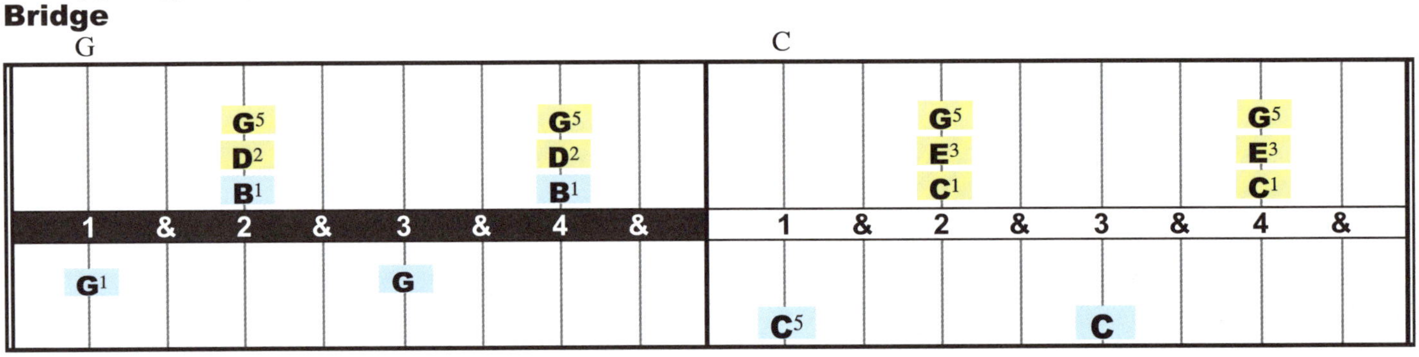

Don we now our gay ap - par - el

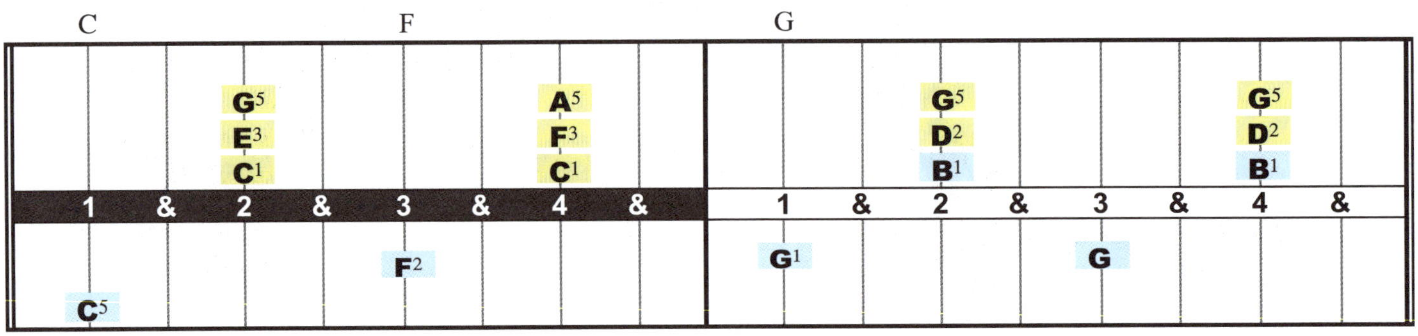

Fa la la la la la la la la

Verse B

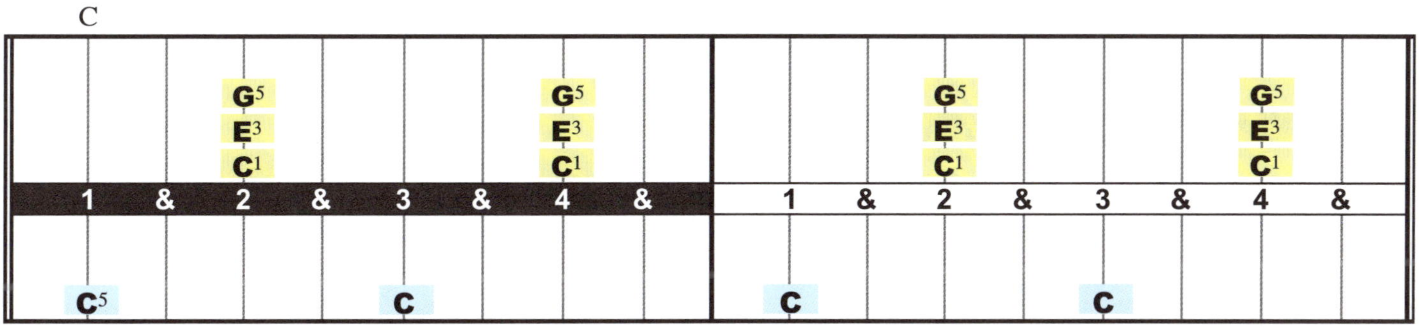

Troll the an - cient yule tide car - ol

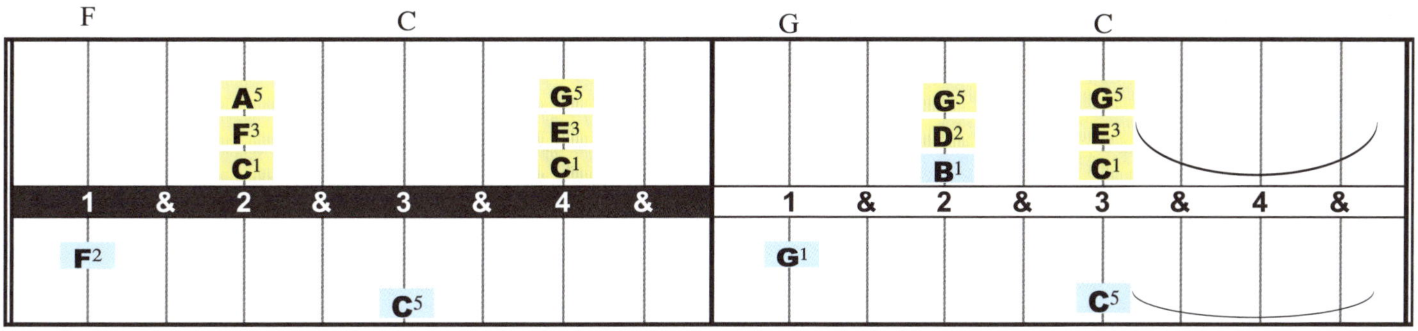

Fa la la la la la la la la

Structure

Verse A - Bridge - Verse B

Verse 2A
See the blazing yule before us
Fa la la la la, la la la la
Strike the harp and join the chorus
Fa la la la la, la la la la

Bridge 2
Follow me in merry measure
Fa la la la la la la la la

Verse 2B
While I tell of Yule tide treasure
Fa la la la la la la la la

Verse 3A
Fast away the old year passes
Fa la la la la, la la la la
Hail the new ye lads and lasses
Fa la la la la, la la la la

Bridge 3
Sing we joy us, all together
Fa la la la la la la la la

Verse 3B
Headless of the wind and winter
Fa la la la la la la la la

1 & 2 & 3 & 4 & 1 & 2 & 3 & 4 &

1 & 2 & 3 & 4 & 1 & 2 & 3 & 4 &

1 & 2 & 3 & 4 & 1 & 2 & 3 & 4 &

1 & 2 & 3 & 4 & 1 & 2 & 3 & 4 &

1 & 2 & 3 & 4 & 1 & 2 & 3 & 4 &

1 & 2 & 3 & 4 & 1 & 2 & 3 & 4 &

1	&	2	&	3	&	4	&	1	&	2	&	3	&	4	&

1	&	2	&	3	&	4	&	1	&	2	&	3	&	4	&

1	&	2	&	3	&	4	&	1	&	2	&	3	&	4	&

1	&	2	&	3	&	4	&	1	&	2	&	3	&	4	&

1	&	2	&	3	&	4	&	1	&	2	&	3	&	4	&

1 & 2 & 3 & | 1 & 2 & 3 & | 1 & 2 & 3 &

1 & 2 & 3 & | 1 & 2 & 3 & | 1 & 2 & 3 &

1 & 2 & 3 & | 1 & 2 & 3 & | 1 & 2 & 3 &

1 & 2 & 3 & | 1 & 2 & 3 & | 1 & 2 & 3 &

1 & 2 & 3 & | 1 & 2 & 3 & | 1 & 2 & 3 &

1 & 2 & 3 &	1 & 2 & 3 &	1 & 2 & 3 &
1 & 2 & 3 &	1 & 2 & 3 &	1 & 2 & 3 &
1 & 2 & 3 &	1 & 2 & 3 &	1 & 2 & 3 &
1 & 2 & 3 &	1 & 2 & 3 &	1 & 2 & 3 &
1 & 2 & 3 &	1 & 2 & 3 &	1 & 2 & 3 &
1 & 2 & 3 &	1 & 2 & 3 &	1 & 2 & 3 &

KEYTAB Note Strip Instructions

The KEYTAB Note Strip fits behind the keys of any piano or keyboard. Cut out the sections below to get started. Scan the QR code or watch the video at this link:

youtube.com/shorts/v9pLOLepY9w?si=slwUvlnVfPHn1c3z

To get instructions on how to install the KEYTAB Note Strip on your piano. You can purchase an official patented two-sided KEYTAB Note Strip at **KeyTabMusic.com**.

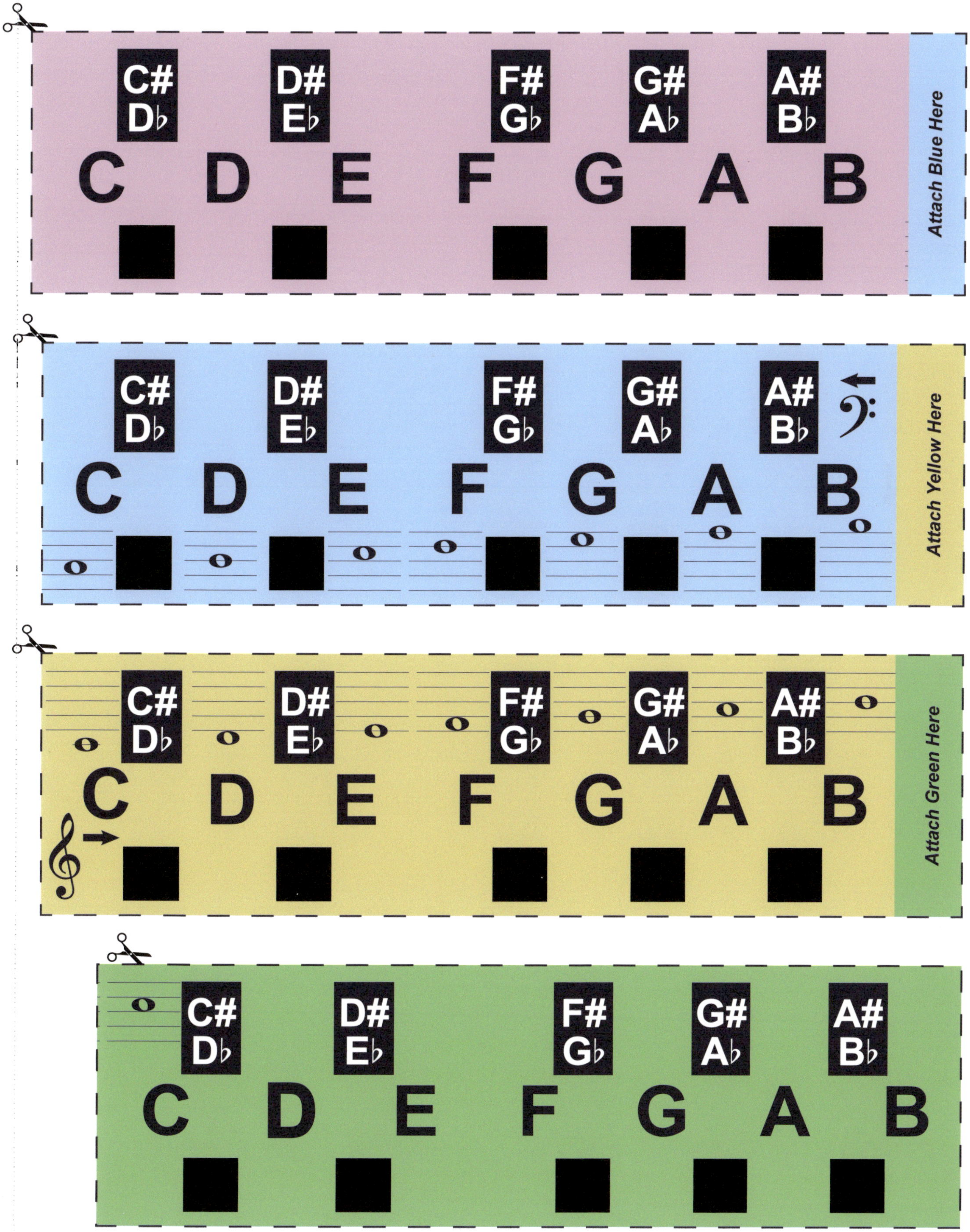
C# D♭
D# E♭
F# G♭
G# A♭
A# B♭
C D E F G A B
Attach Blue Here
C# D♭
D# E♭
F# G♭
G# A♭
A# B♭
C D E F G A B
Attach Yellow Here
C# D♭
D# E♭
F# G♭
G# A♭
A# B♭
C D E F G A B
Attach Green Here
C# D♭
D# E♭
F# G♭
G# A♭
A# B♭
C D E F G A B